Ethnographies of Conferences and Trade Fairs

Hege Høyer Leivestad • Anette Nyqvist
Editors

Ethnographies of Conferences and Trade Fairs

Shaping Industries, Creating Professionals

palgrave
macmillan

Editors
Hege Høyer Leivestad
Department of Social Anthropology
Stockholm University
Stockholm, Sweden

Anette Nyqvist
Department of Social Anthropology
Stockholm University
Stockholm, Sweden

ISBN 978-3-319-53096-3   ISBN 978-3-319-53097-0 (eBook)
DOI 10.1007/978-3-319-53097-0

Library of Congress Control Number: 2017940398

Cover illustration © pixelprof / Getty Images

Printed on acid-free paper

This Palgrave Macmillan imprint is published by Springer Nature
The registered company is Springer International Publishing AG
The registered company address is: Gewerbestrasse 11, 6330 Cham, Switzerland

Acknowledgements

This volume is the product of a series of conversations at the Department of Social Anthropology at Stockholm University over the role and impact of conferences and trade fairs in various anthropological research fields. In 2014, Mia Forrest, Hege Høyer Leivestad, Anette Nyqvist and Hans Tunestad noted that we, despite our diverse research fields and interests, all conducted parts of our respective ethnographic fieldwork at conferences and trade fairs. As we came together to discuss the presence of large-scale professional gatherings in our respective fields, the nature of them, their overlaps and differences, we also began thinking of the possibility of a joint project and an anthology on the topic.

We should like to thank all the contributors to the volume for their hard work and fascinating material. We are indebted to the editors at Palgrave Macmillan who already at an early stage believed in this book.

Many thanks.

CONTENTS

CONTRIBUTORS

Thomas Fillitz is Associate Professor at the Department of Social and Cultural Anthropology, University of Vienna, Austria. His research interests are: global art, (West African) art worlds and art markets. His present, ongoing research concerns the biennial of Dakar. He is the editor (with Jamie Saris) of Debating Authenticity. Concepts of Modernity in Anthropological Perspective (Berghahn).

Melissa Fisher is currently a Visiting Assistant Professor in the Department of Social and Cultural Analysis at New York University and an Associate Researcher in the Department of Social Anthropology at Stockholm University. Her research is situated in the interdisciplinary fields of CMS, American Studies, Urban Studies, Gender and Sexuality Studies as well as anthropology. Her book Wall Street Women (Duke University Press, 2012) ethnographically examines how the first cohort of women in finance enacted market feminisms.

Mia Forrest is a PhD candidate at the Department of Social Anthropology at Stockholm University, Sweden. She is currently completing her PhD thesis on the medical treatment of obesity in Sweden, a project which looks at the epistemology of the obese body amongst these experts. Forrest's background is in anthropology and gender studies and her research interests medicine and embodiment.

Tereza Kuldova is currently a Researcher at the Department of Archaeology, Conservation and History of the University of Oslo and Visiting Senior Researcher at the Department of Cultural and Social Anthropology, University of Vienna, Austria. She is the author of the academic monograph Luxury Indian Fashion: A Social Critique (London: Bloomsbury, 2016) and editor of the volume Urban Utopias: Excess and Expulsion in Neoliberal South Asia (Palgrave Macmillan, 2017).

Hege Høyer Leivestad is currently a researcher in Social Anthropology at Stockholm University. Her research is focused on the intersections of mobility studies and materiality/material culture. Leivestad has done fieldwork in Sweden and Spain and written extensively on the theme of caravanning and mobile homes in Europe.

Anette Nyqvist is Associate Professor of Social Anthropology and Senior Lecturer at the Department of Social Anthropology at Stockholm University, Sweden. Nyqvist's research is focused on issues of power at the nexus of statecraft and market-making. Her ongoing research is on the financial and political strategies of institutional investors and her earlier work was on the financialization and individualization of social security systems.

Hans Tunestad works as a Lecturer at the Department of Social Anthropology at Stockholm University. He received his PhD in 2014 with a dissertation entitled The Therapeutization of Work: The Psychological Toolbox as Rationalization Device during the Third Industrial Revolution in Sweden.

CHAPTER 1

Individuals and Industries: Large-Scale Professional Gatherings as Ethnographic Fields

Anette Nyqvist, Hege Høyer Leivestad and Hans Tunestad

Introduction: Entrance, Registration and Welcome

The venue is a large and anonymous space in the outskirts of the city. Perhaps you took the metro, or parked the car in the adjoin parking lot, later finding your way directed by the signs and cartels announcing the theme of this week's conference event. You are here for a limited time. To meet old colleagues, encounter new ones, scope out opportunities, to find out what is next in the business, gain knowledge, exchange experiences, sign deals and show off. You wait in line to register, are checked off the list, receive your nametag and a catalogue, perhaps a tote bag containing flyers, pens and pins. Everyone who is anyone in your industry is here. In fact, maybe this *is* your industry in a condensed and confined event. These are the people and products, ideas and innovations that your industry puts on display right now. Welcome to the conference or trade fair where industries take shape and identities of professionals are created. Take a

A. Nyqvist (✉) · H. Høyer Leivestad · H. Tunestad
Department of Social Anthropology, Stockholm University,
Stockholm, Sweden

© The Author(s) 2017
H. Høyer Leivestad, A. Nyqvist (eds.), *Ethnographies of Conferences and Trade Fairs*, DOI 10.1007/978-3-319-53097-0_1

1

deep breath, make sure your nametag is properly displayed, straighten your clothes, do not forget to smile and head out to meet your peers. You are hereby invited to enter the conference or trade fair venue, to peek behind the counters, closely inspect the nametags and dig into the goodie-bags.

We have all been there. Tiredly listening to yet another keynote at the business conference or visiting the trade fair in the outskirts of town to look at the latest within interior decoration or higher education. Conferences and trade fairs have during the past decades become a significant global industry in and of itself.[1] And, as we here claim, such gatherings have become key sites for the making and negotiation of both industries and professions. This book is an attempt to make sense of conferences and trade fairs as phenomena in contemporary society. We approach conferences and trade fairs as *large-scale professional gatherings*, understood as organized and particular events, bound by place and time, where a large number of professionals within defined industries assemble to network and to exchange both information and goods. We propose to view large-scale professional gatherings as events where entire industries emerge. And we here use emerge in a dual sense, both as in "come into existence" and as in "become visible." We hold that the presentation and communication, marketing and negotiation of new industry-specific products and ideas at gatherings such as trade fairs and conferences are key moments in the formation of industries. These large-scale professional gatherings are, then, events where such formation is made visible-for industry professionals and ethnographers alike. For the professionals attending their industry conference or trade fair, the gathering is, of course, an important opportunity not only for networking and socializing, but also to gain new knowledge, share information with peers and in general learn the ropes of their respective industry. Large-scale professional gatherings are therefore also events where professional identities are shaped.

Taking a variety of large-scale gatherings as their starting point, the chapters in this book are thus ethnographic encounters that have taken place within the organized boundaries of the conference or the trade fair. From Stockholm to Dakar and from Delhi to New York, these include garment manufacturers, art world professionals, obesity specialists, caravan manufacturers, psychotherapists, responsible investors and feminist businesswomen. From this variety of locations and industries, the authors of this book show that conferences and trade fairs are gatherings where specific industries and professional identities both come into existence *and* become visible.

FIELDWORK IN A VILLAGE OF PROFESSIONALS

As anthropologists increasingly turn their ethnographic gaze to study transnational processes and interconnected, complex communities of elites, experts and professionals, ethnographic practices are adapted. As suggested by Christina Garsten and Anette Nyqvist, conducting ethnographic fieldwork in and of complex organizational settings may require particular skill sets as well as adaptation of traditional ethnographic practices (Garsten and Nyqvist 2013). Calls for "studying up" (Nader 1972), "studying sideways" (Hannerz 1998, 2006) and "studying through" (Nyqvist 2008, 2016; Wright and Reinhold 2011), as well as for "polymorphous engagements" (Gusterson 1997), "following" informants (Marcus 1995), "tag along" fieldwork (Nyqvist 2008, 2013, 2016), "para-ethnographic" and collaborative ethnography (Holmes and Marcus 2005, 2006) and for doing ethnography "at the interface" (Garsten 2009) are all examples of traditional ethnographic practices creatively adapted to be employed in a more complex contemporary setting for anthropological examination.

In this volume, the authors show that large-scale professional gatherings are productive sites for anthropological enquiry. In her chapter here, Anette Nyqvist (Chapter 2) reminds us of the tradition of joining one's informants to the conferences they go to has been long-standing at the Department of Social Anthropology at Stockholm University, where four of the contributors to this volume were trained and others have tight links to. She quotes Professor emeritus Ulf Hannerz of the Department who states that: "Such temporary sites–conferences, courses, festivals–are obviously important in much contemporary ethnography" (Hannerz 2003: 210).

Going with professionals, or following them, to their respective trade fairs or conferences is a way of taking the social dimension of the professional world seriously and considering these gatherings as informative events and excellent opportunities for ethnographic enquiry. Yet, given that these events are nodes in complex entanglements of social relations stretching out in different directions, conducting fieldwork at large-scale professional gatherings entails both the necessity of "being there," taking part in the face-to-face interaction and of situating the particular event in a wider societal context. Including the ethnographic study of trade fairs and conferences into the analysis of professionals' worlds is a way of finding and defining a particular local site and setting within a larger, global, complex space (see Knauft 2006). In line with the notion of "the local" as situationally defined and temporarily spatialized (Garsten and Nyqvist 2013: 15; Strathern 1995) we suggest the trade fair and the conference may be seen as particular, local sites of temporary character. This, we propose, makes the large-scale professional gathering resemble a village of professionals. Complex societies today are characterized by what Hannerz calls "multiplex relationships" (1996: 97), that is, not only the face-to-face interaction between friends and relatives of the small-scale traditional anthropological field, but also by the interaction through professional roles, mediated interaction, as well as sometimes, and increasingly so it appears, surveillance. These are, Hannerz' suggests, primary, secondary, tertiary and quaternary relationships (1996: 95–96).

Large-scale professional gatherings here come to resemble a traditional village with its primary face-to-face interaction, though where the interaction takes place mainly through secondary professional roles, and only for a brief period of time. The notion of a village of professionals is however an oxymoron. If actually investigating a village we may find a few professionals, but no one is ever a professional in the art of being a villager. So when professionals gather together to meet face-to-face–as if in a village–this should not primarily point us towards an analysis of this interaction in terms of primary relations. In other words, we should not think about a large-scale professional gathering on analogy with the kind of small-scale societies that anthropologists excelled in analyzing during much of the twentieth century. We should rather view this interaction as a part of, and analyze it in terms of, a highly contemporary phenomenon, namely the connexionist world, where status largely is a function of mobility, making the personal and professional intimately related. Professionals coming from different places to gather together in order to *connect* through face-to-face interaction are simply following this connexionist logic (Boltanski and Chiapello 2005: 130–131, 155, 362). This is, however, nothing new. Trade fairs date back to, at least, the eleventh century and the European country fair where exchange took place in carnival-like surroundings (Aspers and Darr 2011; Moeran and Pedersen 2011). Aspers and Darr (2011) historically tease out the economic importance such fairs have had, facilitating for instance the development of credit in the fifteenth century, but also the central position of fairs for the establishment and maintenance of networks between traders (2011: 760–761). By emphasizing trade fairs and festivals ongoing "elements of festivity" (Aspers and Darr 2011: 760), "spectacle" (Morean and Pedersen 2011: 4) and the formation of "temporary townships" (Skov 2006: 772–773), these authors have illustrated the historically shaped material and spatial qualities of the fair and the conference in providing not only a space for exchange, but also for the reproduction of hierarchies and sustaining social relationships.

With the notion of contemporary conferences and trade fairs as temporary villages of professionals we wish to emphasize precisely the social formation, structuring and coordination that goes on at these face-to-face professional large-scale gatherings. So, for us anthropologists interested in understanding certain aspects of a specific profession or of professional's work life or perhaps in the knowledge production or sociality of complex organizations, following the professionals we are studying to the conferences or trade fairs that they themselves attend is, we here insist, an important part of our ethnographic fieldwork.

We register, pay the fee, become members, put on the nametag and enter the trade fair or conference to conduct participant observation.

WHERE THE ACTION IS OBSERVABLE

Our ambition with this book is humble. We wish to make a case for the conference or trade fair as, not only suitable, but also highly salient sites for ethnographic enquiry. As the authors of this volume show, conducting ethnographic fieldwork at conferences or trade fairs pave way for compelling anthropological insights into emergent key concerns for specific professions and within particular industries. Anthropologists interested in aspects of professionalization, contemporary work life, knowledge production within specific industries, organizations and markets will most certainly find ethnographic fieldwork at trade fairs or conferences rewarding. These large-scale professional gatherings are condensed, temporary and spatially confined events. Conferences and trade fairs are intense communicative and social gatherings where industry-specific knowledge is shared and negotiated. These gatherings of professionals within certain industries are at that, and since the very beginning, sites for the exchange of both goods and ideas. Large-scale professional gatherings, such as conferences and trade fairs, may be seen as what Garsten and Nyqvist (2013) dub as "hot spots," that is specific sites of connectivity where "complexity is rendered visible and made tangible" (Garsten and Nyqvist 2013: 242). Our claim here is that all these aspects combined makes conferences and trade fairs into compelling events and excellent sites for anthropologists to seek out for ethnographic fieldwork. Some of the complex and interconnected processes observable at conferences and trade fairs that, thus far, have inspired for analytical probing are: the spatiotemporal aspects of these types of events, the role of trade fairs and other large-scale professional gatherings in industry coordination and configuration, in depth and detailed analysis of sociality processes such as networking at conferences, insights into the role and meaning of these type of gatherings and, last but not least, the significance of trade fairs and conferences in processes of exchange.

While social scientists in general have paid little attention to conferences as ethnographic locations per se, the academic literature on trade fairs has been growing in recent years. In various aspects, scholars have clearly shown the value of pointing to historical parallels between the earlier type of "commodity" fair and the variety of fairs one find in contemporary societies. One such parallel are the fairs' spatiotemporal aspects. Trade shows, award ceremonies and similar gatherings are bound by time and space since participants are co-located for a fixed duration of time at a particular site (Hardy and Maguire 2010; Lampel and Meyer 2008), whether the fair is held in the outskirts of town or "taking over" the town itself during a limited period of time (Moeran and Pedersen 2011: 4). As Skov (2006) illustrates particularly well in her studies of the trade fair's role in the fashion industry, fairs are also organized upon principles of periodicity. This periodic character can, according to Moeran and Pedersen (2011: 4–5), be seen as yet another historical trace from the time when fairs were instituted to facilitate large-scale and international commerce and where they–as in many contemporary industries–formed mobile and interdependent networks of fairs.

Trade fairs have in sociological and management studies literature been described as "venues in which the various components of an industry come together" (Aspers and Darr 2011: 759). Such gatherings provide formal and informal opportunities for face-to-face social interaction that allows participants to "share information, establish patterns of domination, and create mutual awareness of a common enterprise" (Anand and Watson 2004; Hardy and Maguire 2010: 1366). A trade fair provides a stage on which buyers and sellers, peers and competitors meet and interact with each other during a limited time, and it has been suggested that a trade fair "has its own culture and unique forms of socializing and networking" (Aspers and Darr 2011: 770). It has further been argued that social encounters at for example a trade fair provide the basis for social networks based on trust and cooperation (Aspers and Darr 2011; White 2002), and that, consequently, such networks "provide a social infrastructure for emerging markets and industries" (Aspers and Darr 2011: 774). Others yet have noted that such gatherings are staged events where social ties are initiated and established and professional identities are created (Aspers and Darr 2011; Power and Jansson 2008).

This recent literature on trade fairs and similar gatherings have, then, well described them in terms of temporal and spatial boundedness and importance for the formation- and sustaining of markets. Networking–in the broadest sense–is as a key term in the existing research on what we here call large-scale professional gatherings.

Coordination and Configuration

In management literature, what we here call large-scale professional gatherings have been described and analyzed as "field-configuring events" (Anand and Jones 2008; Hardy and Maguire 2010; Lampel and Meyer 2008; Schüssler et al. 2014). These events are seen as "temporary social organizations" (Lampel and Meyer 2008: 1026) and arenas where professional and knowledge-based discursive fields are shaped (Hardy and Maguire 2010: 1366; Schüssler et al. 2014). Here people come together and not only "become aware of their common concerns," but also "share information, coordinate their actions, shape or subvert agendas, and mutually influence field structuration" (Anand and Jones 2008: 1037).

However, Moeran and Pedersen (2011) urge us to note the difference between the field-configuring event as it is defined in the management and organization studies literature, and anthropologist Arjun Appadurai's concept of "tournaments of value" (Appadurai 1986: 21), picked up by Moeran (1993) in relation to the advertising industry, and later by Anand and Watson (2004) to understand the fair as "tournament ritual." While management scholars Anand and Jones (2008), by reducing it to a question of terminology, argue for a distinction between field-configuring events and tournament rituals, Moeran and Pedersen show that the conceptual framing of field-configuring event carry similar characteristics (such as spatial, temporal and social boundedness, as well as formal and informal encounters) as the tournaments and fairs of medieval times (Moeran and Strandgaard Pedersen 2011: 21). This volume will not bring this debate any further, but the reader will find that some of the contributors to this book relate and conceptualize with reference to previous research. For example, Forrest (Chapter 5), Fillitz (Chapter 6) and Kuldova (Chapter 8) all take the concept of "field configuring event" to new ethnographic settings, namely among obesity experts, among artists and curators at an African biennial and within the Indian fashion industry, respectively.

There are also central features of the professional large-scale gathering that raise the question of identification. As Aspers and Darr (2011) argue, at these events there are also processes of identification, thus more related to a "spirit of solidarity" and the construction of a "sense of community" (2011: 776). The condensed format of a gathering, making the business in its present phase visible to actors and ethnographers alike, arguably opens up for such processes of identification. This sense of community may even come out of a perceived competitive situation where professionals seek a common ground in identifying themselves in opposition to actors in related businesses–thus actually following a pattern of interaction well known to anthropologists, where people form a common identity in opposition to another group of people (cf. Barth 1969; Evans-Pritchard 1940). That is to say, in this case associations are made and upheld by the professionals at a conference or trade fair in opposition to other fields that they perceive as their competitors. For example, psychotherapists versus psychiatrists or professionals from the responsible investor industry versus "Wall street" (that is more traditional capital investors) or fashion designers versus traditional garment producers.

All in all, field configuration is a complex process that may differ substantially between different fields. To some extent a large-scale professional gathering always has an element of field configuration to it. Indeed, these are events where industries are shaped and professionals created. Pinpointing exactly in what way, and perhaps even to what extent, a specific large-scale professional gathering is a field-configuring event must be an empirical question. Problematizing the idea of field-configuration is also a way of opening up for a discussion about diversity and heterogeneity when it comes to large-scale professional gatherings. This heterogeneity should of course not be overstated. Any large-scale professional gathering has at least a common theme and thus a more or less compulsory point of identification that participants need to acknowledge for their very attendance to make sense. Yet beyond this, a large-scale professional gathering may in some cases appear as a more or less heterogeneous ensemble of activities that goes on more or less simultaneously.

Not all of these gatherings have a ceremony where some kind of price is awarded (Moeran and Pedersen 2011: 20), and even if they do that may be a minor and less well-visited event that not in any sense defines the gathering. Not overstating the ritualistic aspects of a large-scale professional gathering as a whole may thus seem reasonable. These aspects are always there of course: the name tag, the limitations in space and time, and so on. Yet, given the above, these altogether appear as forms of ritualization rather than rituals in a strict sense (cf. Bell 2009).

Networking Engagements

Large-scale professional gatherings such as conferences and trade fairs are particularly important and helpful events for professionals aiming to gain information and knowledge of a specific industry, but these events are also sites for networking, socializing, collaboration and competition (Aspers and Darr 2011). International conferences, trade shows and other types of large-scale meetings typically feature both ceremonial and dramaturgical activities and are opportunities for networking and gaining new knowledge (Hardy and Maguire 2010; Schüssler et al. 2014). That networking constitutes an integral part of many professional's lives today is related to the revolution in information and communication technologies (Castells 1996). Opportunities for networking have, needless to say, been taken to a whole new level the past decades through this revolution. It is therefore, as Aspers and Darr puts it, rather "surprising that in the information age...trade fairs still exist" (2011: 761). What Aspers and Darr see as the reason for the continuing existence of the trade fairs, despite the vast opportunities for networking through other means, is the building of trust through a complex kind of face-to-face interaction that cannot take place otherwise–at least when it comes to the industry they study (2011: 776). However, a common denominator for large-scale professional gatherings in general, related to the idea of these as sites for intensified and complex face-to-face interaction, is that these gatherings constitute condensations of the respective industry. This means that large-scale professional gatherings constitute places where the action is temporarily made observable; places well suited for getting updated on what is going on in a particular industry–and our respective ethnographies support that this is one main reason for participants to go there.

Several scholars have, in various ways, demonstrated and placed emphasis upon the social processes that tie people, objects and ideas into assemblages some of which render into more durable social figurations. When thinking of, and studying, connections and the formation of networks it is of importance to make clear the distinction between the noun *network* and the verb *networking*. Brian Moeran, again, has insightfully pointed to "connections" as the practice and strategic activity typically referred to as networking (Moeran 2005, 2013). "Connections are what people practice, while networks are how they analyze them theoretically," Moeran asserts (2013: 155). Yet another anthropologist interested in the meaning of connections and networking as a practice is Christina Garsten who has shown that, in the world of think tanks, social connections in professional and powerful networks in fact constitute "an economy of connections" where referrals, references and ties "take the form of valuable symbolic capital in a highly competitive and politicized form of exchange" (Garsten 2013: 151). It is, Garsten asserts, "all about ties" (ibid: 139).

While plenty of the socializing at conferences and trade fairs takes place inside the venue, important networking as well as catching up with old friends and colleagues takes place in restaurants, bars and dance floors after hours and outside of the actual meeting space (Aspers and Darr 2011: 770; Nyqvist 2015: 202; Power and Jansson 2008: 433). Informal talk and gossip over food and drink hold important roles not only for socializing and networking at conferences and trade fairs, but also for gaining strategic information of the industry and for signing contracts and closing deals (Aspers and Darr 2011: 770–771; White 1981: 519, 1993: 167). A professional large-scale gathering, then, is arguably "a place where collaborative ties are constructed; these provide means for trust to develop and mutual values and beliefs to become shared and institutionalized" (Aspers and Darr 2011: 772–773). Large-scale professional gatherings, we hold, are events where information and knowledge is exchanged *and* where deals are made and contracts signed–all through social processes and networking.

In the present volume it is Nyqvist, Fisher and Leivestad's chapters that most clearly disentangle the off- and on-site networking. Based on her fieldwork on conferences for actors in the responsible investment industry Nyqvist (Chapter 2) shows that networking has become a significant and formally organized part of the industry conferences. Fisher, in Chapter 3, provides specific insight of professional women's networks–and networking–over time, from the 1950s to the present. By paying close attention to the setting of, and activities at, a particular leadership conference for professional women, Fisher analyzes the contemporary making of white corporate feminine spiritual subjects. Leivestad's chapter (Chapter 7), on the other hand, discusses the caravan and motorhome trade fair as an event where leisure and socializing is formally integrated into its very organization, particularly through the activities taking place at the temporary fair campsite outside the trade fair halls. By emphasizing the processes of intimate family-building that the caravan industry at large resonate with, Leivestad is able to show how the trade fair enables the establishment and maintenance of particularly close connections between industry actors and customers.

As seen in Leivestad's chapter there may be an element of "festival" in any large-scale professional gathering. Meeting up and chatting with old colleagues and friends that you have not seen for a while, that is, informal socializing, perhaps even drinking sessions, and a more or less compulsory party as a sort of concluding event, may all form a part of the trade fair or conference. In this sense, such gatherings may appear as something out of the ordinary, even appearing as a sort of "carnival time" (Moeran and Pedersen 2011: 5). However, we would suggest that the reverse is just as often the case, or even more common. Because more than "carnival time" the large-scale professional gathering in general could be characterized by what we may here call "business as usual time"–that is, conferences and trade fairs are today a more or less integrated part of professionals' ordinary work life. The networking at a large-scale professional gathering is not that different from the kind of networking that is an essential component of many professions today and thus occurs on a regular basis in the lives of professionals. That is to say, participating in a professional gathering is more of just another day at work, reality is not turned upside down, the gathering is merely yet another project in the seemingly endless row of projects where, as Boltanski and Chiapello (2005: 110–111) have noted, each and every person in the end is his or her own main project. This last point is made most relevant in Tunestad's (Chapter 4) and Forrest's chapters (Chapter 5) in their discussions about how psychotherapists and obesity experts respectively become professional beings.

Organization and Meaning of Gatherings

From the recent insights into meeting ethnography, a large-scale professional gathering is not *a* meeting but rather a number of parallel and consecutive meetings (as well as a number of other activities) set in motion by a diversity of actors with different ideas about what they want to do and why they are attending the event (Sanders and Thedvall 2017; Schwartzman 1989).

Meetings are part of the everyday lives of people all over the world. Whatever the reason and whatever the character of the gathering, meeting up is an intrinsically and fundamental human activity and in all cases a social event. For instance, sociologist Erving Goffman views meetings as "social situations," claiming that a meeting is: "Any physical area anywhere within which two or more persons find themselves in visual or aural range of one another" (Goffman 1981: 84). While anthropologist and organizational theorist Helen Schwartzman holds that a meeting is "a gathering of three or more people who agree to assemble for a purpose ostensibly related to the functioning of an organization or group" (Schwartzman 1989: 149). Of relevance here is the insight that systems of meaning are created in and shaped by systems of social relations (Hannerz 1992). A meeting is, then, an organized event with purpose and intention. There are many purposes for humans to meet up. A meeting can have decision-making purposes or aim at the exchange of ideas, experiences or knowledge; and a meeting can have as a goal to solve a problem or to come up with a collective proposal (Goffman 1961; Hymes 1974; Schwartzman 1989). To the intentionality and purpose of meetings Schwartzman holds that meetings are to be seen as a rather distinct type of social event, namely "a pervasive gathering" (Schwartzman 1989: 9), and Goffman too points to the focused character of meetings in his suggestion that meetings are characterized by "focused interaction" (Goffman 1961: 7). From this we gather that meetings not only are intrinsically social events, involving at a minimum two people, but also that meetings are, in one way or another and to various degrees, organized arrangements with particular purpose and intent.

Of most interest to our main argument here is that Schwartzman holds that meetings, in fact, can be seen as "the organization or community *writ small*" [emphasis in original] (Schwartzman 1989: 39). It is, for example, at the meetings of any kind organization that hierarchy and values are made visible and it is at the meetings that structure and culture are realized. The argument is that meetings provide an organization "with a form for making itself visible and apparent to its members" and that this, in turn, "provide individuals with a place for making sense of what it is that they are doing and saying and what their relationships are to each other in this context" (Schwartzman 1989: 9). Suggested here is that what goes on at meetings, activities such as decisions, policy-making or problem solving "are *not* what meetings are about [emphasis in original]" (ibid.: 40). Therefore, scholars making meetings their object of study should reverse their entry point and explore the possibility that meetings, as it were, makes organization visible as well as define, represent and reproduce the social relations and inherent structures of the organization.

Knowledge Exchange

Professional large-scale gatherings are communicative and social events where professionals gather to exchange experiences and knowledge (Goffman 1961; Hymes 1974; Schwartzman 1989). Knowledge is here viewed as "the vast assemblage of persons, theories, projects, experiments and techniques" (Rose and Miller 1992: 177), and "does not simply mean 'ideas'" (ibid.). As such knowledge is seen as something continuously produced and organized, used and diffused. The exchange of knowledge is a key component at conferences and trade fairs, and conversely, professional large-scale gatherings are principal sites/events for the diffusion, sharing and negotiation of new knowledge within industries and for professionals.

Knowledge is, then, here seen as something processual, situational and constantly evolving. Such approach corresponds well with what scholars such as sociologist Karin Knorr-Cetina argues as she stresses the importance of the situation in the production of knowledge. Rather than seeing knowledge as "statements of scientific belief, as technological application, or perhaps intellectual property" (Knorr-Cetina 1999: 8), her definition of knowledge emphasize "knowledge as practiced – within structures, processes, and environments that make up specific epistemic settings" (ibid.). In her view, knowledge is connected to specific settings that can have their own culture; what Knorr-Cetina calls "epistemic cultures" (1999). Another sociologist, Patrik Aspers, claims: "knowledge must be seen as a process and that interpretation and understanding are essential components of knowledge" (2006: 746). Aspers puts forward the notion of "contextual knowledge" to emphasize that knowledge is seen "against a backdrop of a shared lifeworld and it involves interpretation" (Aspers 2006). In fact, knowledge differs from information in that the former is based on interpretation, while the latter is not (Amsden 2001).

From such perspective, knowledge is rarely something stable and unambiguous but instead continuously produced in certain contexts and situations where it evolves in processes of contestation, interpretation and negotiation. Conferences and trade fairs are sites and occasions for such processes. This simultaneous creation and dissemination of knowledge–relevant to the respective fields–constitutes an important reason for here viewing large-scale professional gatherings as field-configuring events where professional identities are created and industries shaped.

ETHNOGRAPHIES OF CONFERENCES AND TRADE FAIRS: AN OUTLINE

In Chapter 2, the first ethnographic, Anette Nyqvist analyzes responsible investment conferences as important meeting grounds for institutional investors, such as pension funds, mutual funds and insurance companies. At responsible investment conferences institutional investors not only seek new knowledge about the responsible investment industry, Nyqvist argues, but they also look for opportunities for collaboration. Her chapter describes how institutional investors socialize and "work the room" at responsible investment conferences in order to find peers to collaborate with. Based on fieldwork conducted in New York and Paris, at small and exclusive professional gatherings of institutional investors and at large, and international responsible investment conferences, Nyqvist's chapter deals with the increased importance of professional networking at industry conferences.

In Chapter 3 we remain in the world of business. Melissa Fisher deals with transnational white corporate spiritual feminism–its rise and growth in the new millennium. Drawing on several decades of fieldwork at conferences and meetings within global women's networks in US and Europe, Fisher interestingly argues that we are witnessing a reorientation of neo-liberal feminism away from a pre-occupation on equality and inclusion in the workplace, towards a series of disparate projects, one of which now includes the importance of individual spiritual and mental well-being. Specifically, the gendered logic of global women's networks has shifted over the past several decades. During the 1990s and 2000s, network leaders moved away from producing meetings centring on women's occupational mobility to a focus on women's empowerment and the business case for gender equality in the economy. Now, turning their attention to producing feminine, feeling and soulful subjects, some leaders seek a different kind of competence in the global economy. Such subjects are purportedly able to successfully navigate an increasing inter-cultural business world composed of powerful actors who traverse traditional distinctions between the global north and south. Conferences are thus training grounds for the making of a new female global elite–women who are increasingly cultural polyglots, able to master dominant and alternative forms of gender, racial and emotional capital.

Hans Tunestad, in Chapter 4, follows that of Fisher's in terms of exploring the role emotions has been given in organizations settings of contemporary western societies. Tunestad investigates the Psychotherapy Fair, a gathering taking place every second year in Stockholm, Sweden. The Psychotherapy Fair resembles a public square where people can gather to meet like-minded and exchange information. But it is also like a market square in that those who have something for sale can here offer their merchandise. Not only are a large number of exhibitors and lecturers invited to the fair, but also the general public. Yet the fair has a hierarchical structure where different fees and registrations enable a more or less intensive participation. The pressure the last decades towards both more cost-effective and scientifically verified treatments has brought about the codification of psychotherapy in a diversity of classifications and manuals, the latter also meaning an increasing number of time limited treatments, occasionally distributed through the Internet, or in the form of self-help books. Altogether this diversification of the psychotherapeutic field has also meant that anyone–from psychiatric institutions to potential patients– can, so to speak, shop around among different therapies, for which the Psychotherapy Fair offers extensive opportunities. All in all, Tunestad argues, the Psychotherapy Fair can be seen as a common public reflection, where the message is that psychotherapy "works."

In Mia Forrest's chapter (Chapter 5), we stay on the medical arena. Forrest's chapter illustrates how conferences on obesity become spaces that produce a medical understanding of obesity. By focusing on a particularly lively debate which continued over several different conferences on obesity in 2010 and 2011 she discusses how the treatment options and pharmaceuticals produces a certain type of medical body and a shared understanding of obesity as a particular kind of disease within the space of the conference. Forrest shows how conferences become important spaces in which obesity experts unite in a specific understanding of obesity as complex medical condition. Conferences are spaces in which expert can discuss their discontent with the lack of treatment for obesity, but also spaces in which they can share their dreams and aspirations for future obesity treatment.

In Chapter 6 Thomas Fillitz enters the world culture of art biennales, and more specifically the biennale of Dakar (Dak'Art). Fillitz approaches the Biennale of Dakar as a "Field-Configuring Event" and argues that a localized study of the Biennale is required in order to understanding the multiple tasks and strategies of the Biennale in the context of the difficult circulations of artworks, artists and art world professionals in Africa, or the aspirations for communication and exchange among these art world actors. The first part of Fillitz' chapter discusses the production of symbolic capital. It is connected to the nomination of selection committees, the importance that is locally accorded to the space of the main venue (the international exhibition), and finally to the role of the prizes that are awarded. In the second part of the chapter he examines the Biennale as constituted of several spaces of encounter and network building.

In Hege Høyer Leivestad's chapter (Chapter 7), the focus lies on the trade fair and its relation to the market. In the geographical peripheries of European cities, trade fairs gather thousands of caravan and motorhome enthusiasts every year; chasing the latest news from the so-called "mobile living" industry. These trade fairs are also spectacular social events, sporting temporary trade fair campsites, as well as a wide range of entertainment and activities. Her chapter asks how we can understand the caravanning trade fair as a market space that challenges the dichotomy between the formal and informal economy. By ethnographically approaching a specific Swedish trade fair, Elmia Husvagn och Husbil (Elmia Caravan and Motorhome), Leivestad looks at how the fair becomes a sphere where the selling of dwellings take place through a continuous reproduction of "like-mindedness" in an environment characterized by close connections between retailers, manufacturers and customers. This chapter thus offers an ethnographic view on the trade fair as a spatially and temporally bounded space that is characterized by notions of intimacy

In the final ethnographic contribution, Chapter 8, Tereza Kuldova takes us to the fashion and garment industry in India. At first sight the Indian fashion industry appears to be split into two distinct and independent social fields with their own rules and status hierarchies. The first centred on the spectacular fashion shows with star designers, celebrities and industrialists filling the glossy magazines, and the second on the textile, apparel and garment trade fairs that barely make it into the news. Kuldova shows us that while we could be seduced by appearance into believing that these two worlds really do not meet, in reality, the fields and the actors within them are profoundly dependent on each other and fully integrated into one value chain. However, this dependence is systematically disavowed by actors within both social fields for different reasons and the split is thus continually re-produced. Kuldova's chapter argues that it is precisely this dynamic of dependence and disavowal that lies at the core of the tense and ambiguous relationship between the social fields centred on fashion weeks and trade fairs and that shapes the industry as a whole, thus also effectively reproducing existing exploitative structures.

NOTE

1. Professionals attending trade fairs and conferences are part of the steadily growing business travel industry, which is a sub-sector of the overall tourism industry. There is a lack of industry statistics and standardized terminology making it difficult to provide accurate numbers about the size and value of the industry. Some see the formation of trade associations as a sure sign of a formation of an industry. If so the birth of the industry for large-scale professional gatherings may be set to 1928 when the International Association of Exhibitions and Events (IEAA) was founded (Rogers 2013: 5). The Union of International Associations (UIA) has been keeping score of large-scale international professional meetings for 60 years. For 2015 they registered that 12,350 large-scale international professional meetings took place in 248 different countries and they predict a 35 per cent increase over the next five years (UIA 2016). In 2015 the global business travel spending was 1.11 trillion US dollars. And industry leaders expect spending to increase significantly in the years to come (http://statista.com).

REFERENCES

Amsden, Alice. 2001. *The Rise of the Rest: Challenges to the West from Late-Industrializing Economies.* Oxford: Oxford University Press.

Anand, N., and Brittany C. Jones. 2008. "Tournament rituals, category dynamics, and field configuration: The case of the booker prize." *Journal of Management Studies* 45(6): 1036–1060.

Anand, N., and Mary R. Watson. 2004. "Tournament rituals in the evolution of fields: The case of the Grammy Awards." *Academy of Management Journal* 47: 59–80.

Appadurai, Arjun. 1986. "Commodities and the politics of value." In *The Social Life of Things: Commodities in Cultural Perspective*, ed. A. Appadurai. Cambridge: Cambridge University Press.

Aspers, Patrik. 2006. "Contextual knowledge." *Current Sociology* 54(5): 745–763.

Aspers, Patrik, and Asaf Darr. 2011. "Trade shows and the creation of market and industry." *The Sociological Review* 59(4): 758–778.

Barth, Fredrik (ed.). 1969. *Ethnic Groups and Boundaries: The Social Organization of Culture Difference*. Oslo: Universitetsforlaget.

Bell, Catherine. 2009. *Ritual: Perspectives and Dimensions*. Oxford: Oxford University Press.

Boltanski, Luc, and Ève Chiapello. 2005. *The New Spirit of Capitalism*. London: Verso.

Castells, Manuel. 1996. *The Information Age: Economy, Society and Culture. Vol 1, The Rise of the Network Society*. Malden, MA: Blackwell.

Evans-Pritchard, Edward Evan. 1940. *The Nuer: A Description of the Modes of Livelihood and Political Institutions of a Nilotic People*. Oxford: Clarendon Press.

Garsten, Christina. 2009. "Ethnography at the interface: 'Corporate social responsibility' as an anthropological field of inquiry." In *Ethnographic Practice in the Present*, eds. M. Melhuus, J. Mitchell, and H. Wulff. Oxford: Berghahn Books.

Garsten, Christina. 2013. "All about ties. Think tanks and the economy of connections." In *Organisational Anthropology: Doing Anthropology in and Among Complex Organisations*, eds. C. Garsten and A. Nyqvist. London: Pluto Press.

Garsten, Christina, and Anette Nyqvist. 2013. "Entries. Engaging organisational worlds." In *Organisational Anthropology: Doing Anthropology in and Among Complex Organisations*, eds. C. Garsten and A. Nyqvist. London: Pluto Press.

Goffman, Erving. 1961. *Asylums. On the Social Situation of Mental Patients and Other Inmates*. New York: First Anchor Books.

Goffman, Erving. 1981. *Forms of Talk*. Philadelphia: University of Philadelphia Press.

Gusterson, Hugh. 1997. "Studying up revisited." *POLAR* 20(1): 114–119.

Hannerz, Ulf. 1992. *Cultural Complexity. Studies in the Social Organization of Meaning*. New York: Columbia University Press.

Hannerz, Ulf. 1996. *Transnational Connections: Culture, People, Places*. New York: Routledge.

Hannerz, Ulf. 1998. "Other transnationals: Perspectives gained from studying sideways." Anthropology and the Question of the Other, special issue, ed. T. Maranhão. *Paideuma* 44: 109–123.

Hannerz, Ulf. 2003. "Being there...and there...and there!: Reflections on multi-site ethnography." *Ethnography* 4(2): 201–216.

Hannerz, Ulf. 2006. "Studying down, up, sideways, through, backwards, forward, away and at home: Reflections on the field worries of an expansive discipline." In *Locating the Field: Metaphors of Space, Place and Context in Anthropology*, eds. S. Coleman and P. Collins. Oxford: Berg.

Hardy, Cynthia, and Steve Maguire. 2010. "Disclosure, field-configurating events, and change in organizations and institutional fields: Narratives of DDT and the Stockholm Convention." *Academy of Management Journal* 53(6): 1135–1202.

Holmes, Douglas, and George Marcus. 2005. "Cultures of expertise and the management of globalization: Toward the refunctioning of ethnography." In *Global Assemblages: Technology, Politics, and Ethics as Anthropological Problems*, eds. A. Ong and S. J. Collier. Oxford: Blackwell.

Holmes, Douglas, and George Marcus. 2006. "Fast capitalism: Para-ethnography and the rise of the symbolic analyst." In *Frontiers of Capital. Ethnographic Reflections on the New Economy*, eds. M. Fisher and G. Downey. Durham, NC: Duke University Press.

Hymes, Dell. 1974. *Foundations in Sociolinguistics: An Ethnographic Approach.* Philadelphia: University of Philadelphia Press.

Knauft, Bruce. 2006. "Anthropology in the middle." *Anthropological Theory* 6(4): 407–430.

Knorr Cetina, Karin. 1999. *Epistemic Knowledge, How the Sciences Make Knowledge.* Cambridge: Harvard University Press.

Lampel, Joseph, and Alan D. Meyer. 2008. "Field-configuring events as structuring mechanisms: How conferences, ceremonies, and trade shows constitute new technologies, industries, and markets." *Journal of Management Studies* 45: 1025–1035.

Marcus, George E. 1995. "'Ethnography in/of the World System.' The emergence of multi-sited ethnography." *Annual Review of Anthropology* 24: 95–117.

Moeran, Brian. 1993. "A tournament of values: Strategies of presentation in Japanese advertising." *Ethnos* 58(1–2): 73–94.

Moeran, Brian. 2005. *The Business of Ethnography. Strategic Exchanges, People and Organizations.* Oxford: Berg.

Moeran, Brian. 2013. "Working connections, helping friends. Fieldwork, organizations and cultural styles." In *Organisational Anthropology: Doing Anthropology in and Among Complex Organisations*, eds. C. Garsten and A. Nyqvist. London: Pluto Press.

Moeran, Brian, and Jesper Strandgaard Pedersen. 2011. *Negotiating Values in the Creative Industries: Fairs, Festivals and Competitive Events.* Cambridge: Cambridge University Press.

Nader, Laura. 1972. "Up the anthropologist: Perspectives gained from 'studying up'." In *Reinventing Anthropology*, ed. D. Hymes. New York: Random House.

Nyqvist, Anette. 2008. *Opening the Orange Envelope. Reform and Responsibility in the Remaking of the Swedish National Pension System.* Stockholm: Stockholm University.

Nyqvist, Anette. 2013. "Access to all stages? Studying through policy in a culture of accessibility." In *Organisational Anthropology: Doing Anthropology in and Among Complex Organisations*, eds. C. Garsten and A. Nyqvist. London: Pluto Press.

Nyqvist, Anette. 2015. *Ombudskapitalisterna. Institutionella ägares röst och roll.* Stockholm: Liber.

Nyqvist, Anette. 2016. *Reform and Responsibility in the Remaking of the Swedish National Pension System. Opening the Orange Envelope.* New York: Palgrave Macmillan.

Power, Dominic, and Johan Jansson. 2008. "Cyclical clusters in global circuits: Overlapping spaces and furniture industry trade fairs." *Economic Geography* 84: 423–448.

Rogers, Tony. 2013. *Conferences and Conventions: A Global Industry.* 3rd ed. London: Routledge.

Rose, Nikolas, and Peter Miller. 1992. "Political power beyond the state: Problematics of government." *The British Journal of Sociology* 43(2): 173–205.

Sanders, Jen, and Renita Thedvall (eds.). 2017. *Meeting Ethnography. Meetings as Key Technologies of Contemporary Governance, Development, and Resistance.* New York: Routledge Studies in Anthropology Series.

Schüssler, Elke, Charles-Clemens Rüling, and B. F. Wittneben Bettina. 2014. "On melting summits: The limitations of field-configuring events as catalysts of change in transnational climate policy." *Academy of Management Journal* 57(1): 140–171.

Schwartzman, Helen B. 1989. *The Meeting. Gatherings in Organizations and Communities.* New York: Plenum Press.

Skov, Lise. 2006. "The role of trade fairs in the global fashion business." *Current Sociology* 54(5): 764–783.

Strathern, Marilyn. 1995. "The nice thing about culture is that everyone has it." In *Shifting Contexts: Transformations in Anthropological Knowledge*, ed. M. Strathern. London: Routledge.

UIA. 2016. The Union of International Associations (UIA) press release for *International Meetings Statistics Report* June 2016 (copy held by authors).

White, Harrison. 1981. "Where do markets come from?" *The American Journal of Sociology* 87: 517–547.

White, Harrison. 1993. "Markets in production networks." *Explorations in Economic Sociology*, ed. R. Swedberg. New York: Russel Sage Foundation.
White, Harrison. 2002. *Markets from Networks, Socioeconomic Models of Production*. Princeton: Princeton University Press.
Wright, Susan, and Susan Reinhold. 2011. "Studying through: A strategy for studying political transformation. Or sex, lies, and British politics." In *Policy Worlds: Anthropology and the Analysis of Contemporary Power*, eds. C. Shore, S. Wright, and D. Peró. New York: Berghahn Books.

URL

Statista.com. The Statistics Portal: https://www.statista.com/topics/2439/global-business-travel-industry/ (accessed November 2, 2016)

CHAPTER 2

Scheduled Schmoozing: Notes on Interludal Practices at Responsible Investors' Conferences

Anette Nyqvist

INTRODUCTION: WORKING THE ROOM

The next item on the conference agenda is coffee: Coffee with milk, a bite size blueberry muffin and 20 minutes intense schmoozing. This is a networking coffee break at a conference for responsible investors' and within minutes hundreds of well-dressed men and women with nametags fill the area just outside of the auditorium. The murmur is loud, the physical space cramped and the atmosphere extremely friendly. People want to meet and look for eye contact. With smiles fixed yet somehow genuine everyone works the room. The rapid exchanges contain an interesting mix of formal introductions, pleasantries, succinct pitches and business cards. People move around the room and talk with each other.

This chapter draws on research conducted within projects funded by: The Swedish Foundation for Humanities and Social Sciences, The Swedish Research Council, The Wenner-Gren Foundations and The Sweden-America Foundation.

A. Nyqvist (✉)
Department of Social Anthropology, Stockholm University, Stockholm, Sweden

© The Author(s) 2017
H. Høyer Leivestad, A. Nyqvist (eds.), *Ethnographies of Conferences and Trade Fairs*, DOI 10.1007/978-3-319-53097-0_2

Some seemingly haphazardly and with whomever happens to appear in front of them by. Others more strategically, aiming for specific individuals whom they have decided to meet and therefore hover around waiting for the opportunity.

Responsible investment conferences, large and small, are important meeting grounds for institutional investors, such as pension funds, mutual funds and insurance companies. At these gatherings institutional investors not only seek new knowledge about the responsible investment industry, they also look for partners to collaborate with.

The focus of this chapter is on what goes on within the organized and formal program of a conference but before, after and in between the conventional knowledge-creation line up of panel discussions and paper presentations. What I here aim to shed light on are the details and patterns of the scheduled schmoozing in the interludes of the responsible investors' conferences that I attend for fieldwork within the responsible investment industry.

A note on definitions is in place here. I use the concept of schmoozing following Merriam-Webster's dictionary's online full definition of "schmooze," which is: "to chat in a friendly and persuasive manner especially so as to gain favor, business or connections" (Merriam-Webster 2016). Webster's New Twentieth Century Dictionary lists, as one of the meanings of "interlude": "Anything that fills time between two events" (Webster's 1977: 958). I here find the notion of interludes more useful than, for instance, the concept of "breaks" as I wish to underline the activities and actual work that fills the time slots between the more traditional events of conferences. Where "break" emphasizes a disruption in and pause of activities, "interlude" points to an activity in between other activities and in significant ways different from these.

This chapter, then, highlights the practice of networking at large-scale professional gatherings such as industry conferences. The premise here is that while socializing was always an integral, albeit informal, part of attending conferences such activities are now recognized as significant and organized elements of the industry conference, equal to the paper presentation or panel discussion. Based on fieldwork conducted at responsible investment conferences in Paris and New York, this chapter deals with what goes on in the scheduled interludes between the conference presentations, seminars and discussions. In sum, I here provide insight into show how investors "work the room" at conferences in order to, as shown in the interviews I have conducted, "find friends" and "join forces" to, as one informant from a large pension fund put it, "have a bigger say" when the institutional investors pressure companies to change.

Institutional Investors

Institutional investors, such as mutual funds, insurance companies and pension funds, are large shareholder organizations commissioned to manage other people's money. These have, in a relatively short time grown in size and scope to now dominate corporate ownership globally (Clark 2000; Drucker 1993; Gold 2010; Hawley and Williams 2000). Mutual funds, insurance companies and pension funds have, at that and over the past decades, come to be influential front figures of the responsible investment industry globally. From the position of being "active" and "responsible" investors, owners and shareholder institutional investors from all over the world adhere to both make money *and* make a difference–to do both well and good.

Institutional investors are fiduciaries and as such they have the responsibility to manage the economic assets on behalf of others. The standards of fiduciary duties generally derive from common law. The specific duties a fiduciary has to follow are based on two fundamental principles, namely: loyalty to the beneficiary and prudence in investing. The duty of loyalty means that the agent is bound by law to act in the best interest of the beneficiary. In most jurisdictions, financial fiduciaries are obliged to manage their beneficiaries' capital prudently and in accordance with the so-called "prudent investor" rule (Freshfields Bruckhaus Deringer 2005; UNEPFI 2009). As fiduciaries then, institutional investors seek change and improvement in the way business is conducted, and many investors therefore actively engage in social and environmental issues with regards to companies in which they own shares. Institutional investors are normative and fostering financial actors that aim to, in their view and for their beneficiaries, better the way companies conduct their businesses (Gold 2010; Hawley and Williams 2000; Nyqvist 2015a, 2015b, 2017; Welker 2014; Welker and Wood 2011).

I hold that institutional investors are interesting, important and intriguing objects for ethnographic enquiry for at least three reasons. First, institutional investors manage other people's money, and that, in itself, sets them apart from traditional financial actors driven by self-interest and makes them interesting entities to investigate. Second, the fact that there has been a shift in ownership on the world's financial markets during the past three decades, by which institutions have emerged as major financial actors that now dominate corporate ownership worldwide, makes institutions not only interesting but also important to study and understand from a perspective of power. Thirdly, institutional investors, acting in the best interest of others, position themselves as financial actors with a significantly different agenda than traditional financial actors. By forwarding notions of what it means to be a fiduciary, institutional investors worldwide have emerged as front figures of the responsible investment industry with an implicit, sometimes explicit, agenda to change the ways of business and finance on a global scale.

COLLABORATIVE CONCERNS

For institutional investors, collaboration is key. Teaming up with other institutional investors is seen as a good way to learn about the industry and it is considered to be a productive strategy to increase ones potential influence on portfolio companies.[1] Institutional investors put a lot of effort into meeting up with and forming alliances with peers; other, often larger and more influential, actors. To this end, key representatives at mutual funds, insurance companies and pension funds often attend industry conferences in order to, as one informant put it, "find friends" (Nyqvist 2015a, 2017). Having asked informants situated at institutional investor organizations, both in Sweden and USA, where they find their potential partners to collaborate with I have found the standard reply to be: "At conferences." "Conferences are the best places to meet peers," says an executive at one of the largest American pension funds. "There are plenty of conferences! I could go to conferences all year round," says a key person at one of the Swedish national pension funds. Another informant, also Swedish, says: "There are conferences all the time. That's where we meet." In interviews people in key positions at Swedish and American pension funds tell me they "find friends" and "meet buddies" at recurring conferences within the responsible investment industry. Informants talk at length about the importance of meeting face to face, of getting to know each other and of sharing experiences and discussing future plans together. That, I am told, is how they find out which other institutional investors around the world they share values with, and who out there works with similar methods. Ultimately, then, meeting at conferences and talking with others in the business is seen as a trust building activity and one that paves way for future collaboration.

CONFERENCE ETHNOGRAPHY

At the Department of Social Anthropology at Stockholm University attending the conferences that one's informants go to have since long been one of many sites to go to while conducting ethnographic fieldwork, as several of the authors in this book here demonstrate. Twenty years ago Tommy Dahlén based much of his fieldwork on the making of the new interculturalist profession on ethnographic material from the emerging industry's conferences (Dahlén 1997). And Professor Ulf Hannerz later concluded that: "Such temporary sites–conferences, courses, festivals–are obviously important in much contemporary ethnography" (Hannerz 2003: 210).

Large-scale professional gatherings, such as trade fairs and conferences, are recurring, but temporary events where people within the same industry meet and exchange experiences, make contacts and do business and hold that these are opportunities for both networking and knowledge-creation (see Chapter 1 in this book for an account of the existing literature). It has been suggested that informal talk and gossip over food and drink play important roles not only for socializing and networking at conferences and trade fairs but also for gaining strategic information of the industry and for signing contracts and closing deals (Aspers and Darr 2011: 770–771; White 1981: 519; 1993: 167). Such networking and socializing often take place after hours and outside of the actual gathering, program and venue (Aspers and Darr 2011: 770; Lampel and Meyer 2008: 1026; Schüssler et al. 2014: 141). My aim with this chapter is to point to the fact that the networking and socializing at industry conferences increasingly has become part of the official and scheduled conference programs (Nyqvist 2015a: 202).

I will, in what follows, first make an initial note of some of the unifying elements at the responsible investment industry conferences that I have attended so far. I then show that at these conferences, the socializing and networking typically seen and described as informal, after hours and outside of the gathering are, in fact, scheduled into the official conference program. I here propose that the shift of networking from an informal to a formal and scheduled part of the conference program underline the crucial importance of collaboration in the responsible investment industry. I then pay specific attention to what, in fact, goes on at the scheduled networking interludes at responsible investors' conferences. The ethnographic examples I present in this chapter deal with: first, the scheduled networking interludes *before* and *in between* panel discussions and paper presentations; here often coffee and pastry is served. And second, I provide ethnographic examples from networking sessions within the official program but *after* the last presentation of the conference day; here typically drinks, alcoholic beverages of different kinds, are offered. I shall then move on to describe and discuss some of the characteristics of the scheduled networking interludes as a whole. My interest in doing so lies in providing insight into the who, how, where and whats of scheduled schmoozing at industry conferences.

I have for some years now studied the practices and policies of institutional investors that position themselves at the forefront of the responsible investment industry. Between 2010 and 2014 I paid particular attention to what the four Swedish National Pension funds and their Ethical Council as well as one of Sweden's largest insurance companies did and said as "active" and "responsible" investors and shareholders (Nyqvist 2015a, 2015b, 2017). From 2014 until just recently my focus shifted to studying how the four largest state pension funds in USA, namely CalPERS and Calstrs in California and New York State Common Retirement Fund and New York City Pension Funds in New York, formulate and communicate their respective responsible investment guidelines. As part of my ethnographic fieldwork on the responsible investment practices of Swedish and American public pension funds I "followed" (Marcus 1995), or rather "tagged along with" (Nyqvist 2016), people that work at the largest pension funds in both countries to some of the main conferences that they themselves make specific effort to attend. I have, over the past six years been to numerous responsible investment conferences large and small in Stockholm, Sweden, Paris, France and Washington DC, California and New York in the US. The illustrative examples included in this chapter come from observations at three large-scale international conferences of the responsible investment industry, namely PRI in Person in Paris in September 2011, RI Americas seventh Annual conference in New York in December 2015 and PRI 10 years in New York in April 2016.

UNIFYING ELEMENTS

There are various, some seemingly minor but still significant, forms of connectivity that bind professionals at a large-scale gathering together. One obvious marker of connectivity at conferences is the mandatory nametag with at least information of the bearer's full name and affiliation. The conference name, date and logo are often also printed on each name-tag. Pre-printed, the nametag that is handed to the participant upon site registration is placed in a plastic holder and either pinned to the clothes or hung around the neck of all meeting participants who consequently then are shaped into a collective, united group. Sometimes also information of the role, function or expertise of the conference attendee wearing the nametag is printed on it. So, while the nametag in a sense unites meeting participants, variations in, for example colours of the tag, lettering or string, can signal distinctions between meeting participants (Entwistle and Rocamora 2006: 741; Nyqvist 2015a: 199).

At the conferences I go to for fieldwork, sometimes different colours of the string in which the nametag dangles indicate a specific function in the industry, other times ones position or affiliation is simply written on the nametag. The distinctions can, for example, be to specify whether the person works as an asset owner, an investment manager, a research provi-der or perhaps a professional service partner. The point here is that, within the ongoing unifying and connecting going on, clear categorization and boundary-setting also occur. The various workings of the nametag indi-cate that the conference or the trade fair is also a place for what has been called "intense boundary work" (Aspers and Darr 2011: 775).

Another unifying, and therefore potentially differentiating, element is the dress code. At the industry conferences I attend for fieldwork on the role of pension funds in the responsible investment industry, the com-monality of the grey suit is conspicuous. The conference attendees are typically men in suits and ties, with shiny shoes and briefcases. Over the past six years, and two research projects, I have met only a few exceptions: a handful of women in suits and scarves and a couple of daring men in suits but without ties. There is virtually no exception from the formal business attire in the rooms where I conduct fieldwork. Grey suit, soft coloured shirt and matching tie is the undisputable and unifying dress code of this world. The appearance in this field is, in fact, so dominant that I developed a methodological concept based on it. I often think of my fieldwork strategies for this research in terms of "following suit" (Nyqvist 2013: 99). I find that "to follow suit" in the sense of to "go along with," to "imitate" is a fitting description of what this type of fieldwork entails. Not least when I find myself strategically networking, wearing a grey dress and business cards in hand, in interludes at investor conferences. There and then, the notion of "follow suit" seems both appropriate and descriptive, as it not only describes a form of engagement during fieldwork, but also points to a unifying feature among the people in this field.

SCHEDULED NETWORKING

In recent years the object to encourage and enable conference attendees to mingle and meet is evident also in the use of technological aids. An e-mail sent out to all of us registered to attend the seventh annual Responsible Investor conference in New York in December of 2015 informs us specifically of the RI NYC conference app, and the benefits of downloading it:

> This year we will have an app to support our event. Delegates will be able to network with each other directly via a messaging service, customise your own schedule for the event, submit a question to our panelists and download various material provided by our sponsors and speakers. All from your own device at the conference using the individual wifi code located on the back of your delegate badge. To get the most out of RI Americas please use the following links to download the "RIA 2015" app from your relevant app store. (Excerpt from e-mail received December 2, 2015)[2]

I find it, here at the onset, appropriate to evoke Brian Moeran's call for a clear analytical distinction between the noun and the verb network (Moeran 2013). This quite obvious and simple point is both important and useful. My interest is in networking as a strategic action and practice and more specifically how the links and connections of a network are created and forged. "Connections are what people practice, while networks are how they analyze them theoretically" (Moeran 2013: 155). Christina Garsten (2013) too insightfully considered the importance of contacts and networking practices. Stating: "It is all about ties," Garsten shows how systems of relations and contacts form structures of both power and knowledge (2013: 139).

Reviewing the agendas of the responsible investment conferences that I went to between 2010 and 2016 it is striking how the act of networking is given prominence in the organization of these large-scale professional gatherings. There is, for example, usually a networking session scheduled into the program after the obligatory registration and before the first speaker. Sometimes this item in the conference program reads simply: "registration and networking," while other times it may say: "networking breakfast" or "morning networking break." Typically, throughout the day's conference program, there are interludes for coffee and lunch between the sessions of talks, discussions and seminars. At the industry conferences I go to these items are listed as: "Networking coffee break," "Networking lunch break" and, after the day's last speaker: "Networking cocktail party" or "Networking drink reception." According to the conference catalogue of PRI in Person 2011,[3] this is where: "...all PRI signatories meet, collaborate and learn with peers." It is where: "PRI signatories, industry experts and thought leaders" meet and engage in "thought provoking sessions and peer-to-peer dialogues" and, says the conference catalogue, "there is plenty of time to network."

Now, come, let us grab a coffee or a drink and dive in to the scheduled and strategic schmoozing at the interludes of responsible investment conferences.

HAVING COFFEE

Thursday morning in Paris, September of 2011. This is my first major responsible investor conference. There is coffee, registration and networking in the vast lobby of the hotel where the conference is. With coffee in my left hand and nametag pinned on to my grey dress I shake hands, demonstrate how to pronounce my last name, elevator pitch my project and hand out business cards. Less than 30 minutes into the morning networking interlude I am all out of cards and retreat to a corner to take notes. They read: "Exchange of cards! Very fast and determined!"

It is 8.35 AM and the "Networking Breakfast" at RI Americas has just begun. In the reception area just outside the auditorium at the large business media corporation that hosts the conference, yoghurt, smoothies, muffins, bagels and fresh fruit is tastefully presented at a large table. People move around the table placing breakfast items on small plates that quickly fill up. Coffee and tea is served in the corner of the large room. With plate in one hand, coffee in the other and notebook with pen under one arm I approach a small group of people that I actually recognize from home. The Scandinavians at the conference seem to have gravitated towards each other and are now standing close together. The top executive from a Swedish institutional investor shows the head of the Norwegian Pension Funds Ethical Council a clip from his latest video on his phone. We all engage in a discussion on communication strategies and the use of external consultants. We introduce ourselves, although several already know each other. We exchange business cards and then the group dissolves. I want to put the plate and cup down to take notes and move over to one of the few high tables in the room. A woman in grey business suit, a shade darker than mine, immediately approaches me. She also puts her plate and coffee down, stretches out her hand and introduces herself. We exchange cards, drink our coffee, eat our muffins and talk, for a minute or two, about major changes in the industry. And then we move on for further schmoozing.

Back to PRI in Paris and to the scheduled networking between sessions there. Panel discussions last an hour and after each there is a 30 minutes coffee break in the Gran Foyer just outside of the auditorium. Here several hundreds of conference attendees crowd around the many Nespresso machines and tables with pastries. The sound of large institutions engaged in small and swift talk resonates in the Gran Foyer. There are two UN-people talking to an IMF person, representatives from OECD and the World Bank are engaged in conversation, executives from several European pension funds have gathered around an executive from one of the larger American pension funds.

"Isn't it amazing!" a man I have changed cards with already in the morning suddenly exclaims beside me. He looks around the room. "This is such a great social networking opportunity!" he asserts before he mingles on. I lock eyes with another man in suit, we smile, introduce ourselves, exchange cards and begin to talk. I ask him what he makes of the networking. He replies: "It's good to meet people face-to-face. Everything else is online, but actual meetings are invaluable."

During the next networking coffee interlude I see a familiar face: a key actor from the Swedish National Pension Funds and someone I have interviewed several times back in Sweden. He is satisfied, says he is here to meet people, reconnect with some of those he spoke to at last year's conference. He explains: "Everyone here has the same problem. It's good to know that you are not alone. It's good to come out sometimes."

At RI Americas in New York in December 2015 it seems, at one point, that the networking interludes are more appealing than the panel discussions in the auditorium. During one of the two-day conference's mid-morning networking interludes scheduled to take place between 10.40 and 11.00 many attendees linger on, do not return to the auditorium but instead stay out in the networking area to keep mingling. I, on the other hand, have taken my seat in the audience in front of the stage where a prominent panel is introduced. There are noticeably less people in the auditorium now compared to before the networking coffee and the intense murmur from the coffee room is heard through the closed doors when this next panel discussion begins. Heads turn towards the closed door and I suspect others, not just me, inside the auditorium wish they had crabbed another cup of coffee and continued the networking instead of listening to the panel discussion. The two different activities are now clearly in competition.

After a few years of conference ethnography I have now acquired new skills in how to schmooze and work a room. I have observed how people scan the crowd, zoom in on someone in particular and approach that person in a determined yet amicable and courteous manner, smile ready and business card at hand, and I now sometimes do the same in order to establish contact with informants otherwise difficult to get to. I have found that the networking interludes at industry conferences can be strategically used to introduce oneself, pitch the research project and swiftly follow-up with a request for a meeting or an interview. Here at the industry conference there is ample opportunity for direct connection and personal interaction with key actors, without middle managers, assistants, secretaries and other gatekeepers blocking or delaying initial contact.

HAVING DRINKS

After the last panel discussion of the last day at RI Americas in New York the organizer takes the stand and thanks everyone for attending and engaging in the two days of discussion and networking. "But" he adds with a smile, "we've done some research on conferences and it turns out alcohol facilitates human networking. So welcome out to the drinks!" There are applauds and laughter as the auditorium empties and the adjacent reception area quickly fills up. The conference item "5.20–7.00 Networking Cocktail Party" has begun. A make shift bar, where wine by the glass and beer in bottles is served, has replaced the coffee and cake counter from earlier in the day. Waiters now walk around with trays of American flavoured bite size food items such as mini-burgers and "pigs in blankets."[4] The sound level rises quickly, the networking is louder now and the room is so crowded it is difficult to move about. But I have now learned how to better work the room and I zigzag smoothly between people. Beer in hand since this is less likely to spill, in the crowded room, than a glass of wine. I make sure my nametag, hanging from a red string around my neck, faces outwards. I spot a group of people from a particular industry organization that I have been wanting to get in touch with. I approach them with a smile and leave them less than 10 minutes later with their respective business cards and promises of interviews within the next couple of weeks.

Earlier, in 2011, as I arrive at the conference hotel for the PRI in Person in Paris late on the night before the two-day conference I over hear two men talking in the elevator up to the room on the 22th floor. They talk about the afternoon, and it seems there was an invitation-only asset owner's networking event I did not know about, much less was invited to. The two men in the elevator discuss it. One attended, the other did not. "I went shopping a bit. How were the cocktails? Did you go?" "Yes, I did. But I drank water." They both nod. "I got to talk to one of the Swedish National Pension funds though," he adds with a smile. So from this I understand that while that networking interlude was not part of the ordinary conference program it was organized as a networking session for a particular category of conference attendees as an official and exclusive part of their program.

The very last item on the agenda of the PRI in Person 2011 is a networking gala where the room is literally spinning. Everything and everyone rotates slowly in the glassed pavilion to where the conference has now moved. Spotlights sweep slowly over the mingling mass of conference attendees in the otherwise dimly lit room. Nametags still intact, glass in one hand, small plate with artful appetizers in the other hand–the conference networking continues, if not escalates. Everyone is in motion; the food and drinks too. The tables are not tables per se but platforms hanging from the ceiling, they are filled with colourful and delicious-looking hors d'oeuvres and they turn slowly round and around. The bars are on wheels and pushed around by waiters to different locations in the large room. Everything and everyone is circulating, working through the room in an intense industry conference networking extravaganza.

Recently, at the PRI 10 year celebration conference in New York 2016 there is both a networking drink reception followed by a sit down dinner where the networking takes place around the large round tables that seat 12 people. The venue for this conference is far from the ordinary conference venue. This conference is fancy and festive and takes place at 583 Park Avenue on Manhattan's Upper East Side. The building was originally, and still occasionally, a church but tonight it is mundane yet high end with uniformed bellhops outside, a line of staff waiting to take coats inside. The conference is in The Ballroom; a spacious room with high ceiling, an enormous chandelier and the tall organ pipes behind the stage as reminder of the other purpose of the locale. Everything lit in blue and purple. This is the conference room, we are all seated at the tables and here the program is not interrupted by networking. Instead the presentations take place back to back and the networking begins after the last speaker as we are all asked to "please move downstairs."

When I come downstairs to the drink reception the sound level in the already packed room is alarming and the schmoozing in full swing. People stand shoulder to shoulder in the blue-lit room. I do what everyone else are doing; I grab a glass of white wine from one of the silver trays carried by uniformed waiters with left hands on their backs and eyes steady straight forward and I begin to slowly circle around the room. By now I recognize many from the industry and am myself a familiar face to some. I move around the room like everyone else. I pause and talk to people that I have met at other conferences and others that I have subsequently interviewed. I take a few steps and then halt to introduce myself to someone I have wanted to meet. We exchange pleasantries and business cards and move along. Next someone who wants to meet me stops me to introduce himself. And so the networking continues until dinner is served upstairs and the networking proceeds around the large round tables in the Ballroom. Here brief intro-ductions with handshakes and business card-exchanges go around the table and before dessert a couple of people have pulled out their calendars to book meetings with each other. Someone has to leave to catch a train, someone else to relieve the baby-sitter. Departing phrases vary from longer: "So nice meeting you. Good luck with everything. Shoot me an e-mail and we'll schedule something." To the brief: "Call me." Accompanied by a hand gesture of holding a phone to the ear and then. "Bye!"

NETWORKING THE ROOM

In what follows is a summarizing discussion of the rooms for scheduled networking at interludes, who the networkers are, and insights into how the networking is done.

The Room

The scheduled networking sessions in between presentations and discus-sions, the "Networking coffee breaks" for example, typically take place at in between spaces at the site of the conference. During the interlude between two sessions attendees leave the auditorium where the talk was but since conference organizers do not want them to stray too far the "Networking coffee" is served in the area just outside the auditorium. Oftentimes the scheduled networking interlude prior to the day's first talk or discussion is also held in such adjacent space while the networking after the day's last session–the drink reception–is in a different space, still in the proximity but perhaps downstairs or next doors.

There is a slow but steady movement in the room as people move around to talk to each other. Small, careful steps from one individual to the next, from one group to another close by. People circulate, not necessarily in circles but in constant and consistent motion. The exceptions are the lines. Static formations in more or less straight lines. Here, in front of the coffee machines or the bar or, as it were, outside the women's restroom, the networking continues as people strike up conversation while waiting in line. And, there are lines to individuals. I have, at several occasions during the scheduled networking interludes, found myself queuing up to introduce myself and exchange a few words with a particularly prominent person attending the conference. And while standing in line interesting interactions take place.

The Networkers

The overarching sense at these large-scale international conferences is that "everyone is here"! Top executives from all the world's largest institutional investors, key actors from the world's most renowned transnational organizations such as UN, OECD, IMF and World Bank, and executives from the business community as well as leading so-called service providers of the industry all typically attend what has come to be the main conferences of the industry.[5] There are a few immediate and conspicuous observation one makes regarding who is in the room: One is that the majority are men, another that they are all in suits–all men and most of the women attending, and yet another observation is that the suits are all grey. The room is coloured in shades of grey with a few hints of discrete colour in ties, scarfs, shirts and blouses. Usually one or two individuals stand out from the grey colour scale in a bright coloured tie or scarf. As a collective the appearance of the responsible investment industry is, as stated earlier in this chapter, formal and grey. To this there are some seemingly minor but significant forms of connectivity that bind the professionals at any conference together. Take for example the nametag. And the pre-printed, nametag that is handed to the participant upon site registration is placed in a plastic holder and either pinned to the clothes or hung around the neck of all meeting participants who consequently then are shaped into a collective, united group. The nametags, of course, unite conference attendees as a group but small variations in for example colouring or lettering also signal distinctions and set different categories of attendees apart. At the responsible investment conferences sometimes differences in professional roles are made visible on the nametags. At PRI in Person for instance attendees are classified as either asset owners, asset managers or service providers. This information is seen to facilitate efficient networking and eliminate spending time talking to "wrong" people.

The Networking

The speed and efficiency of the networking during the scheduled interludes of responsible investors' conferences is striking. It is an intense and efficient, bordering on aggressive networking. Eyes scan the room at chest levels, quickly reading nametags. If something on the nametag, name or affiliation, seems interesting there is immediate eye contact, a quick flash of a smile, initial verbal contact and formal introduction. The "Hellos," "His" and "How are yous" echo in the room. After initial and affable contact, one's affiliation and position, aims and missions are dealt with: "I work with such and such at this and that and I'd really like to get more involved in something or rather. How about you?" The polite small talk and nice chit chat that follow is focused entirely on business and the apparent objective is to find partners with whom one might initiate a business relationship. What goes on is in fact rather swift talk than small talk. Small talk implies irrelevant but nice conversation about the weather or some other innocuous topic but here the small talk is more to the point and with a purpose. There is an eye-smile-talk-hand-motion because then, immediately following the smile and initial dialogue, sometimes during, there is the ritual of the business card exchange. Some have their card out already at "Hello," others reach into their pocket during the introduction, and yet others hand over their card as a parting motion as they already look for new nametags in the immediate vicinity. I have elsewhere called this "organizational speed dating" (Nyqvist 2015a) and if there is no immediate promise of a new affair or potential partnership you politely but quickly move on to the next person. In the beginning I was out of business cards already by the first afternoon coffee break of day one at the conference but I have, since then, learned to carry extra stacks of cards with me to these gatherings.

Wrapping Up the Schmoozing

The scheduled networking interludes at responsible investors' conferences are obviously an integral part of the work that institutional investors do. It needs to be. In order to join forces and, as it were, amplify their voices (Nyqvist 2017), institutional investors around the world collaborate with other institutional investors with similar values, missions and methods. This is in order to put pressure on the companies in which they invest and all ultimately to, in accordance to their fiduciary duties, act in the best interest of their beneficiaries. One important site for institutional investors to meet and get to know potential collaboration partners is at the numerous industry conferences. At responsible investment conferences attendees, of course, learn about the latest news, debates and topics within the business. This is typically done, as at any industry conference for professionals, through attending the scheduled presentations, panel discussions, breakout sessions, seminars and workshops. At responsible investment conferences, I quickly noted, the socializing and networking too is a formal and scheduled activity and official part of the conference program, in par with the panels and talks. It is in the scheduled networking interludes before, during and after the speeches and presentations that institutional investors meet peers and potential partners in intense and strategic mingling and schmoozing sessions. The many organized networking sessions at the investors' conferences, I suggest, must therefore be seen as having significance equal to, if not more, the more traditional conference items such as paper presentations and panel discussions.

Front Stage, Back Stage and Outside

In this chapter I hold that the shift of networking from an informal to a formal and scheduled part of the conference program emphasize the significance of collaboration in the responsible investment industry. Erving Goffman's (1959) conceptualizations of front stage and back stage evoke interesting food for thought here.[6] Goffman famously applied the metaphors of "drama" and "performance" to the understanding of human social organization and his analysis of how context, position and purpose shape the way individuals engage with each seems pertinent here.

Goffman defines three different "regions" connected to each performance: the front stage, the back stage, and the outside. The front stage is where the individual displays and enacts the performance before observers; it is the official, arranged, intentional and rehearsed performance (1959: 17–30). But the relative aspects of the regions, or positions, in Goffman's analysis are brought to the fore with the "back region" or back stage. This is defined as "a place, relative to a given performance, where the impression fostered by the performance is knowingly contradicted" (1959: 112). It is back stage, behind the scenes and away from the view of the audience that "stage props" and personal items are kept, where costumes are adjusted, masks removed and characters abandoned. It is back stage that the performer relaxes and "drops his front" (ibid.). Back stage, therefore, is dependent upon and connected to the front stage and relates intimately to the performance that is enacted before an audience. Now, the socializing over coffee or drinks at professional large-scale gatherings typically take place in what could be described as "back stage," that is apart and separate from the formal conference program. Such informal talk over food and drink play, however, significant roles both when it comes to gaining new information and knowledge of the industry and in meeting peers and business partners (Aspers and Darr 2011; Lampel and Meyer 2008; Schüssler et al. 2014; White 1981, 1993). What then, happens when the "back stage" is brought "front stage"? Is there a new back stage? If so, where is that and what goes on there? In his work Goffman introduces a third less used position, namely "the outside" (1959: 135). In Goffman's analogy and analysis, this region refers to all that does not relate to the performance. Undoubtedly many interesting things happen with relevance to human social organization happen here but for Goffman what goes on "outside" is irrelevant for the study of a particular performance and the social organization and interactions of the individuals performing it. This, the, leads me to think that if the informal schmoozing that at other professional large-scale gatherings take place back stage, is moved up front and centre stage at the conferences that I attend as part of my fieldwork, perhaps the *real* back stage–where fronts are dropped and guards let down–is subsequently moved, as it were, outside.

Be that as it may, for my purposes the intense scheduled networking is sufficient enough. I leave each conference with a full notebook but drained of energy and with slight jaw cramps from all the smiling. My own stack of business cards are gone and exchanged for a pile of new ones for me to follow-up on. Industry conferences, then, are not only the best places for the institutional investors to meet peers. It is, it turns out, also excellent site for the ethnographer to meet informants.

I have here wanted to call attention to the fact that practices of networking increasingly are seen as core parts of the professional conferences of certain industries. The scheduled networking items of the conference programs are, as I have here shown, often considered as important as the paper presentations and panel discussions of the industry conference. I can only recommend any ethnographer interested in a certain profession or industry to register for that industry's annual conference, stack up on business cards and set out to conduct participant observation among conference attendees both seated in the auditoriums and schmoozing in the interludes.

NOTES

1. Meaning companies in which the institutional investors are shareholders.
2. Copy of e-mail held by author.
3. Copy of catalogue held by author.
4. A piece of hot dog wrapped in dough.
5. My selection of RI industry conferences to attend had an economic rationale. Several of the other major annual gatherings proved to be too costly for me to go to. It is not unusual for a conference registration fee within this industry to be anything from $1000 and up. I have over the years downloaded enough conference agendas and attendance lists to note that the key actors in the industry typically attend both the costly and the not so expensive gatherings, and the agendas are organized in similar ways.
6. I have in earlier work on methodology and the topic of access made use of and discussed this same conceptualization of Erving Goffman's, see (Nyqvist 2013: 98–99).

REFERENCES

Aspers, Patrik, and Asaf Darr. 2011. "Trade Shows and the Creation of Market and Industry." *The Sociological Review* 59(4): 758–778.

Clark, Gordon L. 2000. *Pension Fund Capitalism*. Oxford: Oxford University Press.

Dahlén, Tommy. 1997. *Among the Interculturalists. An Emergent Profession and Its Packaging of Knowledge*. Stockholm Studies in Social Anthropology, 38. Stockholm: Stockholm University.

Drucker, Peter F. 1993. *Post-Capitalist Society*. Oxford: Butterworth-Heinemann Ltd.

Entwistle, Joanne, and Agnés Rocamora. 2006. "The Field of Fashion Materialized: A Study of London Fashion Week." *Sociology* 40(4): 735–751.
Freshfields Bruckhaus Deringer. 2005. *A Legal Framework for the Integration of Environmental, Social and Governance Issues Into Institutional Investment. UNEP Finance Initiative.* October 2005. Genève, Switzerland: United Nations Environment Programme Finance Initiative.
Garsten, Christina. 2013. "All About Ties. Think Tanks and the Economy of Connections." In *Organisational Anthropology: Doing Anthropology in and Among Complex Organisations,* eds. C. Garsten and A. Nyqvist. London: Pluto Press.
Goffman, Erving. 1959. *The Presentation of Self in Everyday Life.* New York: Anchor Books.
Gold, Martin. 2010. *Fiduciary Finance. Investment Funds and the Crisis in Financial Markets.* Cheltenham, UK: Edward Elgar Publishing.
Hannerz, Ulf. 2003. "Being There…and There…and There!: Reflections on Multi-Site Ethnography." *Ethnography* 4(2): 201–216.
Hawley, James P., and Andrew T. Williams 2000. *The Rise of Fiduciary Capitalism. How Institutional Investors Can Make Corporate America More Democratic.* Philadelphia: University of Pennsylvania Press.
Lampel, Joseph, and Alan D. Meyer 2008. "Field-Configuring Events as Structuring Mechanisms: How Conferences, Ceremonies, and Trade Shows Constitute New Technologies, Industries, and Markets." *Journal of Management Studies* 45(6): 1025–1035.
Marcus, George E. 1995. "Ethnography in/of the World System: The Emergence of Multi-Sited Ethnography." *Annual Review of Anthropology* 24: 95–117.
Merriam-Webster's Learner's Dictionary. 2016. "Schmooze." *Merriam-Webster.com* http://www.merriam-webster.com/dictionary/schmooze (accessed October 13, 2016).
Moeran, Brian. 2013. "Working Connections, Helping Friends. Fieldwork, Organizations and Cultural Styles." In *Organisational Anthropology: Doing Anthropology in and Among Complex Organisations,* eds. C. Garsten and A. Nyqvist. London: Pluto Press.
Nyqvist, Anette. 2013. "Access to All Stages? Studying Through Policy in a Culture of Accessibility." In *Organisational Anthropology: Doing Anthropology in and Among Complex Organisations,* eds. C. Garsten and A. Nyqvist. London: Pluto Press.
Nyqvist, Anette. 2015a. *Ombudskapitalisterna. Institutionella ägares röst och roll.* Stockholm: Liber.
Nyqvist, Anette. 2015b. "The Corporation Performed. Minutes from the Rituals of Annual General Meetings." *Journal of Organizational Ethnography* 4(3): 341–355.

Nyqvist, Anette. 2016. *Reform and Responsibility in the Remaking of the Swedish National Pension System. Opening the Orange Envelope.* New York: Palgrave Macmillan Books.

Nyqvist, Anette. 2017. "Talking Like an Institutional Investor. On the Gentle Voices of Financial Giants." In *Politics and the Corporate World*, eds. C. Garsten and A. Sörbom. Cheltenham, UK: Edward Elgar Publishing.

Schüssler, Elke, Charles-Clemens Rüling, and Bettina B. F. Wittneben. 2014. "On Melting Summits: The Limitations of Field-Configuring Events as Catalysts of Change in Transnational Climate Policy." *Academy of Management Journal* 57(1): 140–171.

UNEPFI. 2009. *Fiduciary Responsibility. Legal and Practical Aspects of Integrating Environmental, Social and Governance Issues Into Institutional Investment. A Report by the Asset Management Working Group of the United Nations Environment Programme Finance Initiative. July 2009.* Genève, Switzerland: United Nations Environment Programme Finance Initiative.

Webster's Dictionary. 1977. "Interlude." *Webster's New Twentieth Century Dictionary Unabridged*, 2nd ed.. Cleveland, OH: Collins World Publishing.

Welker, Marina. 2014. *Enacting the Corporation. An American Mining Firm in Post- Authoritarian Indonesia.* Oakland, CA: University of California Press.

Welker, Marina, and David Wood. 2011. "Shareholder Activism and Alienation." *Current Anthropology* 52(3): 57–69.

White, Harrison. 1981. "Where do Markets Come From?" *The American Journal of Sociology* 87(3): 517–547.

White, Harrison. 1993. "Markets in Production Networks." In *Explorations in Economic Sociology*, ed. R. Swedberg. New York: Russel Sage Foundation.

CHAPTER 3

White Corporate Feminine Spirituality: The Rise of Global Professional Women's Conferences in the New Millennium

Melissa Fisher

INTRODUCTION: DRUMMING AND BUSINESS

On October 1, 2014, approximately 700 well-groomed professional man-agerial class women and a few men–primarily from Europe–gathered in the ballroom of the InterContinental Berlin. Also present were a smaller number of female executives from Shanghai, Abu Dhabi and other emerging centres of finance in the global south, and a few men. I, in the midst of fieldwork, joined them for the *Global Women International (WIN) Conference*–"a three plus day leadership learning extravaganza for company executives, managers, entrepreneurs and artists alike." The conference agenda explained:

> The WIN Conference is the 17th in a series of visionary global leadership forums inspiring women worldwide. WIN represents a collective leadership journey for the modern women. The WIN approach starts with our "World" – giving a global overview; then moves on to "Work" – conscious

M. Fisher (✉)
Department of Social and Cultural Analysis, New York University,
New York, NY, USA

© The Author(s) 2017
H. Høyer Leivestad, A. Nyqvist (eds.), *Ethnographies of Conferences and Trade Fairs*, DOI 10.1007/978-3-319-53097-0_3

business, professional and career issues; and finally it's all about "You" – your personal growth and wholeness and the journey to lead the way and make a difference in the world. For transformation to be lasting, in the world, at work and in our lives, WIN believes that change needs to happen in a paradigm of global awareness and with an understanding of our inter-connectedness, authentic expression and integration of the feminine values. Collaboration, receptivity, empathy, intuition, integrity, resilience, sensory awareness, beauty and grace become central as we evolve our leadership.

On the first day of the conference, we slowly filed into a softly pink lit ballroom as a medley of 1970s disco songs played in the background. Soon Kristin Engvig, the conference organizer and leader, welcomed us. She introduced Doug Manuel and his male drummers from Sewa Beats, a Swiss-based management company that teaches business skills through participatory "traditional" African drumming. Manuel is white and British. Some of the drummers are also white and British; others are black and West African. Manuel began by instructing each of us to find a drum, called a Djembe, under our seats. For the following hour, he and his bandmates taught all 700 women how to play various rhythms. Drumming, Manuel explained, provides a way for women to locate their "authentic feminine selves." It allows them "to communicate" with their senses and to "be present."

In the new millennium, elites have claimed feminism. White celebrity feminists and their corporate-sponsored events seem to be everywhere today. Suddenly, female executives are championing women's empowerment and authenticity. And, unlike many of their predecessors, who did not publicly speak out against the male establishment, these executives have joined the ranks of corporate leaders in advocating social change, including gender equality. But their target is not changing the workplace per se. Rather, for example, in her 2013 book *Lean In*, Sheryl Sandberg promotes a purportedly new form of corporate feminism urging women to initiate an "internalized revolution." Notably, new-age business feminists, like Kristin, advocate creating social and political change through inner spiritual transformation. On and off stage, she urges women to "realize their own authentic feminine selves" in order to "take responsibility as world citizens" in "times of global uncertainty."[1] That is, bringing about change does not necessarily require changing the social structure of institutions or organizing public protest. First and foremost, women must get in touch with their soulful, grounded, feminine selves. And doing so requires engaging with and appropriating the spiritual practices of racialized "others" and their objects–including, in this case, West African drummers and their drums. As such, contemporary corporate feminist spiritualism represents a neo-colonialism typified by white people discovering themselves in other, often brown people's places and practices.

This chapter is about transnational white corporate spiritual feminism–its rise and growth in the new millennium. Drawing on several decades of fieldwork in global women's networks, particularly participant-observation at meetings, I argue that this new focus on spiritual and mental wellbeing is one of a series of disparate projects that make up contemporary neoliberal feminism (Fisher 2006, 2012; Rottenberg 2014). Specifically, the gendered logic of global women's networks has shifted over the past several decades. During the 1990s and 2000s, network leaders moved away from producing meetings centering exclusively on women's occupational mobility to a focus on women's empowerment and the business case for gender equality in the global economy (Fisher 2010, 2012). Now, turning their attention to producing feminine, feeling and soulful subjects, some leaders seek a different kind of competence in the global economy. Such subjects are purportedly able to successfully navigate an increasing inter-cultural business world composed of powerful actors who traverse traditional distinctions between the global north and south. As Kristin explained to me, "spirituality" is the next way of doing business. Conferences like WIN are thus training grounds for the making of a new female global elite of cultural polyglots, able to master dominant and alternative forms of gender, racial and emotional capital (Elliot and Urry 2010; Ramos-Zayas 2012). Kristin's call for feminine spiritual values in business can be understood as participating in what sociologist William Davies has called "the happiness industry," which he argues includes a move towards the new religion of our age: our emotions (Davies 2015).

Spirituality, Feminism and Neoliberalism

Once relegated to the cultural fringe, the New Age movement is at the cultural centre of the United States in the new millennium, with a billion-dollar book industry, popular shows such as Oprah, and meditative practices being offered in offices. Businesses in Europe are also applying spiritual principles to management (Goldsschmidt Salamon 2005). Increasingly spiritual gurus participate in major transnational elite events. In 2014, for example, a Buddhist monk taught meditative and relaxation techniques to billionaires, pop stars and executives alike at Davos, the annual gathering of the world's (mostly white, mostly male) elite in Switzerland (Davies 2015). Gathering of Kristin Engvig, Doug Manuela and other spiritual leaders at WIN later that year is indicative of a shift in emphasis amongst elites (men and women) from previous decades. Global elites are increasingly preoccupied with mental and physical wellness, and the fundamental belief that a happy, relaxed, empowered executive is able to solve the world's problems.

The social and cultural study of increasingly mobile global elites is relatively under-researched (McKenna et al. 2015). However, ethnographic work on elites and their organizations in business and finance is growing (Fisher 2012, 2015; Garsten and Nyqvist 2013; Holmes 2013; Jansson 2016; Zaloom 2006). There is also an emergent literature on large-scale professional meetings and conferences and the ways such events shape particular industries, identities and forms of knowledge (Aspers and Darr 2011; Sanders and Thedvall 2017). However, relatively little, with the exception of my earlier work on Wall Street women's meetings (2010, 2012), has been written about the gendered dimensions. Indeed, we know very little in terms of what really goes on at meetings like WIN that are explicitly focused on women, business and spirituality.

Feminist scholars working in a range of disciplines have centred on the rise of white spiritual feminism, the female neoliberal spiritual subject and a flourishing marketplace of spiritually oriented businesses owned by women in the global north and south (Crowley 2011; Freeman 2013; Moreton 2007). Recently sociologist Nicole Aschoff explores the "new prophets of capital" including Sheryl Sandberg who push the capitalist work ethic as the antidote to gender inequality (2015). She joins a growing number of scholars writing on Oprah Winfrey, Elizabeth Gilbert of *Eat, Pray, Love* fame and the self-help industry writ large (McGee 2007). However, with the exception of my earlier work on the rise of "professional-managerial class new age feminism" amongst Wall Street women in the 1990s and early 2000s, there is no in-depth ethnographic account of the merger of workplace spirituality and feminism in global women's business networks in the new millennium (Fisher 2006).

During the past several decades, an academic feminist discourse about how to characterize the relationship between feminism and capitalism has emerged. Scholars have increasingly drawn attention to the ways that neoliberal capitalism has co-opted feminism (Eisenstein 2009; Fraser

2009). They have coined a variety of terms for this new type of feminism including post-feminism (McRobbie 2009), market feminism (Fisher 2012; Kantola and Squires 2012), and transnational business feminism (Roberts 2012). These depoliticized feminisms, it is argued, focus primarily on promoting individual women's empowerment; they do not pay attention structures of power and inequality.

Scholars have also increasingly critiqued such perspectives for conceiving of both feminism and neoliberalism as singular entities that can be neatly stitched together – in an overarching, linear and often epochal account of the present (Newman 2012). As I argue in my book *Wall Street Women* feminist ideas and practices have never been completely co-opted by capitalism, nor has feminism entirely transformed financial firms, actors and practices. Indeed, as I show, ethnographically focusing on a single group of Wall Street Women, from the 1950s to the present, allows us to understand how the women themselves reflect on, critique, and sometimes re-work the changing relationship between markets and feminism over time (Fisher 2012). Drawing on anthropologist Aiwa Ong's work on "mobile assemblages," feminist sociologist Janet Newman suggests that we think of neoliberal feminisms as mobile assemblages, comprising technologies, techniques, and practices that are appropriated selectively as they come into contact with "local" politics and cultures (Newman 2012: 163).

WHITE CORPORATE FEMINIST SPIRITUALITY AS ASSEMBLAGES

This chapter examines the production and performance of WIN annual meetings as assemblages of white feminine corporate organizational privilege and being, suggesting that such a framework is critical to understanding the ways global elite women reproduce and justify their power. It does so by examining key dimensions of WIN meetings, and suggests that once these are made more visible we are able to reflect upon more complex processes of the relationships between feminisms and neoliberalisms, and whiteness and spirituality. At the WIN conference specifically, there are three ethnographic elements of, or windows on, these emergent assemblages.

First element is the physical place, space, and bodies where the conference took place: The luxury InterContinental Hotel, in a global and gentrifying city, Berlin, with 700 women. Understanding how whiteness, feminism and privilege are inscribed here includes understanding how

WIN executives bring various components together to produce the conference at the hotel: all the steps in organizing, producing, and marketing such an event–from conceptualizing the theme, to deciding upon the city and hotel, as well as the choreographed arrangements of the subject positions and players it draws in–executives, artists, healers, sound technicians and, of course, paying attendees. Following the organizers at WIN meetings, for example, we see that Kristen and her team assemble technologies, bodies, subjects, practices and affects to produce white corporate feminist spirituality. They arrange, appropriate and sometimes alter elements of white professional women's practices from the past several decades. Concretely, WIN events include the more standard talk of how to be successful in the business world and the more recent spiritually infused discussions of new-age gurus and healers.

Second aspect: the female elite self as a spiritual project. We can interpret Kristin's calls for women to engage in making world change via an "authentic" self as the move that I have been describing towards white feminine spiritual affect. Following the participants, for example, we can see that women, mostly but not exclusively white, attend WIN conferences for a set number of days to learn how to embody authentic, feminine leadership styles associated with being a successful global corporate citizen. In events foregrounding authenticity, spirituality, and femininity, they enact performances of white corporate female spirituality–learning an orientation of openness and intuition. In marketing materials and in person at the conference they hear talk of "exploration, listening, observing and making discoveries (WIN Conference Book, 3)." Kristin's "welcome letter" to WIN, for example, is peppered with new-age terms and concepts. Drawing on the new-age notion of life as a journey, for example, she even suggests that the conference itself is a collective journey for the participants. The trajectory of this journey moves from the global to the local, the macro to the micro. It links women's ability to effect change in the world to their ability to be thoughtful feminine beings.

And, the third window: Here I contextualize contemporary corporate feminist spirituality within the broader history of capitalism, particularly the rise of neoliberalism (Harvey 2005; Ortner 2011). I am particularly interested in considering the ways it participates and animates broader trends in capitalism. These include the financialization of everyday and organizational life (Martin 2002). It also entails the turn towards mindfulness and spirituality in the workplace as well as the new premium that corporations put on feminine ways of performing in the economy (e.g. being risk averse) after the 2008 financial crisis (Fisher 2012; Freeman 2014).

Historical and Multi-Ethnographic Methods

In this project, I take a historical, global and multi-sited ethnographic approach that pays attention to people (particularly female elites and their networks, including WIN) and ideas (about gender, business, spirituality and feminism) circulating within and across institutional and national borders over time. I focus primarily on a WIN conference I participated in and attended in Berlin in October 2014. I interpret my WIN experience against the backdrop of several decades of archival research and fieldwork on Wall Street women and their networks. I first began engaging in field-work on Wall Street women in the mid-to late 1990s. I conducted formal interviews with over 100 women as well as fieldwork and archival research in the Financial Women's Association (FWA) and 85 Broads. Between 2006 and 2008, I returned to conduct follow-up with the cohort. Given some dramatic events that followed 2008, namely the financial crisis–I returned to the field in 2010 (Fisher 2012).

During the past six years, I have continued to meet with the first generation of women and tracked the careers and networks of professional women following in their path (Fisher 2015). This has included conduct-ing in-depth research on WIN based in Switzerland. To this end, I have attended and participated in several WIN conferences, including the 2014 one in Berlin and a more recent smaller meeting in NYC in 2016. I have also interviewed Kristin Engvig, the founder of WIN; Doug Manuel, the founder of SEWA Beats; and other WIN participants.

Engaging in the ethnography of elite women's networks has enabled me to observe the real changes in the lived, on-the-ground practices of women and their networks, including the ways they incorporate spiritual-ity and feminism. Moreover, an historical ethnographic approach provides insight into the emergence of white corporate spiritual feminism. The remainder of this chapter thus maps out the history of the emergence of what I am calling "global corporate feminist spiritual-tainment events" with a particular focus on shifts in professional women network's gen-dered, spatial and self-making tactics from the 1950s to the present, a period of transformations in global markets, businesses and elites. I then turn my attention back to the WIN conference and the making of white corporate feminine spiritual subjects.

WOMEN'S NETWORKS: 1950s TO 2015

I attended WIN's 17th conference–*Magnificent Leap of Change*–from the morning of Wednesday October 1st to the afternoon of Friday October 3rd, 2014. During my three-day stay I could not help but reflect upon changes I had observed in professional women's networks and their events over the past several decades. Indeed, such networks, in the United States and Europe, have grown and transformed dramatically from mostly locally or nationally based organizations to international ones like WIN. When I first started doing archival research and fieldwork in the early 1990s in the Financial Women's Association (FWA), the FWA was by and large a locally New York City-based network of predominantly women on Wall Street. Their meetings took place several times a week, most often after work in office meetings rooms throughout Manhattan or, on occasion for breakfast, before work. They focused predominantly on how to be a successful businesswoman in finance.

From its inception in the late 1950s until the 1990s, the FWA was essentially the only "game," in other words network, for Wall Street women in town. This began to shift during the 1990s. Financial firms developed their own internal affinity networks as part of their business's diversity efforts. Firms, for example, such as Heritage J.P. Morgan developed policies to define and deal with forms of difference. By the late 1990s, early 2000s, part of that effort included the participation of more than 18,000 employees worldwide in approximately 90 affinity groups at the now named J.P. Morgan Chase. Although the women's network boasted one of the largest memberships (around 5,000), a wide range of networks based on race, cultural heritage, gender, sexual orientation, disability and other defining criteria began sprouting up (Fisher 2006: 231).

In parallel, external Wall Street networks began to emerge during this period as well. In 1997, Jesse Jackson, for example, founded the "Wall Street Project," a division of his Rainbow/PUSH coalition based in New York City, articulating a strategy of incorporating African-Americans and other excluded groups into the stock market (Ho 2009: 23). Two years later, in 1999, Janet Hanson, president and CEO of Milestone Capital, the country's first women-owned firm to specialize in managing institutional money market funds, created a women's spin-off of Goldman Sachs named 85 Broads. 85 Broads was a play on the physical address of Goldman Sachs, 85 Broad Street in Manhattan, and the colloquial term "broad" for women. The group was composed of women who worked at

Goldman Sachs and an increasing number of female executives who had left the firm either by being fired (due to cutbacks) or on their own volition, particularly in the wake of the fall of the dot-com era and 9/11 (Fisher 2006: 210).

In contrast to the FWA's weekly events in New York City and annual trips to a foreign country, 85 Broads tended to stage all day conferences every few months for its members in various global cities: New York City, San Francisco, Frankfurt, Tokyo, and London. Unlike many FWA meetings that historically examined being successful in finance and business, 85 Broad events centred on key questions, echoing the focus of Oprah Winfrey's self-styled program, such as *What is Your Destiny?* and *What's Your Gift?*. Indeed, it was not altogether surprising that in an interview with a younger member of 85 Broads in 2001, the woman called Janet Hanson "Oprah-esque." Janet, like "Oprah," she told me, "is all about asking what's your life about and what our destiny means to us."

The notion of the self, articulated in 85 Broads was not exclusively or even necessarily about mastering a successful business personae; it was primarily about an essence to develop and cultivate. This version of success as self-fulfilment and empowerment, embodied in new-age thought, promises compensation for the degradation of or loss of work. Its roots are in the 1950s American definition of success as the product of a partial retreat from work into a familial world of leisure (Traube 1992: 74). Thus, by the early 2000s, professional women were being told and learning that one, in part, trades career advancement for the emotional fulfilment of finding one's inner gift and destiny. Thus, at the *What is Your Destiny?* event, women like Jackie Zehner, a Goldman Sachs trader, spoke about their desires to leave Wall Street and to do something to help women–for example make movies about women. 85 Broads women's articulation about finding their "destiny" revealed the ways a new generational network of business women elaborated a more new-age exploratory type of self-work ethic (Heelas 2002: 80). Here, we can see professional work becoming more broadly defined and being "taken to provide the opportunity to 'work' on oneself; to grow; to learn ('the learning organization'); to become more effective *as a* person" (du Gay 1996 cited in Heelas 2002: 83).

This was not an isolated event or phenomenon. Notably, as Kimberly Crowley argues in her book on white spiritual feminism, beginning in the 1980s and 1990s, white middle class women increasingly turned towards new-age practices (such as yoga, crystals and drumming) and away from active feminist protest (Crowley 2011: 7). Thus, at the dawn of the new millennium, 85 Broads began to infuse a more contemporary exploratory self-work ethic with what in 2006 I called "an emergent professional-managerial-class new age feminism" (Fisher 2006: 234). New events, produced by Janet Newman, 85 Broad's owner and creator, represent the beginning of the infusion of new-age spirituality into professional women's networks ideologies and practices. And an ocean away, at the very same time, Kirsten Engvig was growing her own network into an international corporate spiritual feminine empire.

WIN seeks to tap primarily into an emerging market of elite female and millennial consumers. While the racial composition of the FWA and 85 Broads was largely white, the portrait of WIN attendees reflects what I call the new global white corporate female elite–a group of mostly women who do not quite resemble what, up until quite recently we imagined when we conjured up a version of the well-off in the United States and Europe (Lind 1995; Mills 1956). They are not all born into rich families. They are not all white. And they are not all from the Global North (Kahn 2012). They are, however, part of what George Lipsizt refers to as the "white spatial imaginary," an imaginary which structures feelings as well as social institutions. Notably, it "does not emerge simply or directly from the embodied identities of people who are white. It is inscribed into the physical contours or the places where we live, work, and play and is bolstered by financial rewards for whiteness" (Lipsitz 2011). Indeed, as we shall see, the WIN conference can be read as an elaborate training for professional women into a new global culture and embodied way of being of white female elite-ness and privilege.

White privilege is inscribed in the Berlin Intercontinental, the site of the 2014 WIN conference. The hotel is part of the luxury InterContinental Hotels brand. It is situated directly in the centre of Berlin, a rapidly gentrifying city. The surrounding neighbourhood is composed of old monuments, shiny new apartment buildings and high-end restaurants. The hotel is an enclosed enclave unto itself. It boasts 34 business meeting rooms, a conference room "pavilion," along with the usual high end hotel amenities–luxurious rooms, buffet breakfasts, a gym, swimming pool and even a spa. However, what is so remarkable about the InterContinental Berlin is its very lack of remarkability. As soon as I entered the lobby, the morning of October 1st, I felt as if I could easily be in the lobby of any number of five star hotels in cities like New York, London and Berlin. Indeed, such hotel settings very deliberately generate a certain global, ahistorical, sanitized setting that aims to divorce the guests from the very political, economic and racial contexts that create them. And yet, I felt uncomfortably aware that everyone–from the doorman to the receptionist–treated me with the kind of classed "deference and personal recognition" sociologist Rachel Sherman writes about in her ethnography on *Luxury Hotels* (2007). When I first arrived at the hotel, the receptionist was unable to find my reservation. She apologized profusely, offering me endless complimentary cappuccinos in one of the bars. Finally, after several female WIN executives intervened on my behalf, I was given the electronic keycards to a luxury suite: One key allowed me entry to an elevator to the floor of special suites; the other was for my hotel room. After unpacking a bit and redoing my make-up I went back downstairs to attend the opening *Big Bang Ceremony*. I ended up sitting at a table of white women from Sweden and Chicago. A few minutes into the drumming I turned to one of the women from Chicago to ask if she had noticed that the men on stage were black from Africa and most of audience was white from the United States and Europe. She looked around and said no. The performance of gender and race was unnoticed, while being performed in plain sight.

WIN conferences are part of a longer history: Gatherings of the global elite have been taking place for decades. Perhaps the most well-known gathering place for international business, government, media and cultural leaders is the Davos World Economic Forum held annually in Switzerland for nearly four decades (Rothkopf 2008). Davos, like many elite national and international gatherings, is, by and large still a boy's club. In 2013, only 17 per cent of the delegates were women, a number that has remained static despite a new policy that requires that companies must send one woman for every four men (Roy 2013; Sörbom and Garsten 2015).

But WIN is also part of a new era of professional women's conferencing that is sweeping across the United States and Europe as well as parts of the Global South. Since the 1990s, in part a response to the dearth of women at such events, a number of own global elite women's conferences have been established throughout the world. The Global Summit of Women was established in 1994. Its most recent meeting, which took place in June 2015 in Paris, France was entitled *Women: Redesigning Economies, Societies*. Major entertainment companies have also recently embraced the concept of professional women's conferences. As part of her tenure at Newsweek/The Daily Beast, Tina Brown hosted "Women in the World" conferences with luminaries and celebrities like Hillary Clinton,

Oprah Winfrey and Angelina Jolie in attendance. Politico now hosts "Women Rule" events (Valenti 2014). Notably, the emergence of these types of conferences reflects the rising cultural consumption of certain brands of feminism. They are also part of the advent of more performative and entertainment oriented forms of feminism. This includes Beyonce's reclaiming of feminism at the 2014 MTV Video Music Awards.

In the past several years, a newer type of women's conference in the United States has emerged fusing ideas about women's leadership with new-age ideologies and wellness practices. In 2012, Omega launched the *Omega Women's Leadership Center*. Notably, the purpose of the cente is to "Promote women's leadership by convening, inspiring, and training women to lead from their own authentic voice, values, and vision" (www.eomega.org). During the same year, Chantal Pierrat founded Emerging Women and Emerging Women Live based in Colorado "in order to support the integration of consciousness and business" (www. emergingwomen.org). Claire Zammit of the *Feminine Purse*, Elizabeth Gilbert of *Eat, Pray, Love* fame, and numerous other women will be keynote speakers at the upcoming 2016 Emerging Women Conference in San Francisco. And, of course, there is WIN which has been in existence in Europe for nearly two decades.

GLOBAL CORPORATE FEMINIST SPIRITUAL-TAINMENT EVENTS

So far, we have only glimpsed the leading edges of these new WIN types of conferences, what I am coining *global corporate feminist spiritual-tainment events*. These new types of events are defined by the following central three features: First, they are *theme-o-centric*, by which I mean everything that goes on and in place within the conference is contained within a particular, over-arching and notably new-age theme. The theme of the 2014 WIN conference was, for example, *Magnificent Leap of Change*. Second, they are *immersive*. Women's professional events in the 1980s, 1990s and even early 2000s lasted a few hours in the morning or afternoon, or at most a weekend. By contrast, WIN conferences place over several days. They are total immersive events, more similar perhaps to the Erhard Seminars Training (EST) happenings of the 1960s, than anything else–though arguably seemingly less restrictive. And they take place in (mostly) white enclaves–gated communities like the Berlin Intercontinental or Omega Retreat in Rhinebeck, New York. Third, and perhaps most importantly, as discussed in the beginning of this chapter, they are *assemblages*. Kristen and her team assemble technologies, bodies, subjects, practices and affects. They arrange, appropriate and sometimes alter elements of professional women's practices from the past several decades. On a concrete level this entails composing events that include the more standard talk of how to be successful in the business world and the more spiritually infused discussions of new-age gurus and healers. They also use professional artistic groups to enliven trainings and to help women to experience themselves and their bodies in particularly sentient ways. These professional healers and artists are, I argue, a new type of entrepreneur on the global conference circuit. Hailing from a range of places including Cameroon, Ireland and Nigeria, they engage in new forms of emotional labour that synthesize healing, spirituality and business (Freeman 2014).

The first day of the 2014 WIN conference I attended began with not one but two events: The Big Bang–the drumming session spearheaded by Doug Manuel and his team from Sewa Beats; and the "opening cere-mony" which included "an inaugural concert" composed of pianists, opera singers and a professional "storyteller." Doug Manuel and the Sewa Beats are thus part of the performative turn that has taken place in business since the early dawn of the new millennium. As Manuel explained to the conference attendees, engaging in drumming allows women to access their "authentic feminine selves." Kirsten and her team have thus choreographed the conference to start with drumming so that participants can effectively find the potential of the feminine managerial body. The apparent warm glow of female connection and practical ecstatic efferves-cence of West African drumming and other bodily techniques are not mere side shows or simply entertainment at such events. Rather they are deeply performative and central to creating white feminine corporate subjects. They are an affirmation of collective identity amongst WIN participants of their elite white professional-managerial identity vis-à-vis other groups. Specifically, white professional-managerial women partici-pate in new-age corporate feminism in part to negotiate the long, complex and many would say failed political alliances with women of colour. As Karlyn Crowley argues in her book *Feminisms' New Age*, "spiritual prac-tices 'allow' white women to live out fantasy unions with women of color that have been disrupted in the public, feminist, and business sphere" (Crowley 2011: 8). WIN's drummers and other new-age performers filter new-age ideas that personalize, racialize and translate them for the mostly female global elite audience that participates at WIN.

Drumming at WIN conferences make the women participants more visible to themselves as caring, authentic feminine bodily selves. Moreover, their emotional performances represent the white caring, sentient, saviour-like feminine body as the reservoir of knowing how to conduct oneself and business in the current economic moment. In the wake of the 2008 financial crisis, elite white men and their reckless, testosterone-fuelled behaviour were viewed as the source of the economic meltdown. Women and their natural, risk averse, stance towards finance were seen as the possible saviours of the economy. This did not result in huge personnel changes–more women (in terms of numbers) have not necessarily been elevated to high-ranking positions on Wall Street. However, financial executives are now charged with purportedly being more responsible for managing the economy through a purportedly more risk-sensitive feminine-like approach. Bodily techniques, such as drumming, produce soulful, grounded white feminine-like bodies–bodies able to traverse the recklessness and enormity of post-financial crisis life.

Engaging in new-age practices is not the only way WIN makes new female managerial subjects. WIN also teaches women to appreciate and consume classically high forms of cultural art forms. Notably, the Big Bang opening was followed by an "inaugural concert" that in contrast to the drumming was performed by opera singers and flutists. Traditionally, elites (men and women) in the United States and Europe understood themselves to be part of a group. They defined themselves by what they excluded and by their own distinct culture including the appreciation of opera. However, as Shamus Kahn (2011) points out in his ethnographic work on new boarding school adolescent elites, today's elite differ from their predecessors: "What marks elites as elites is not a singular point or view or purpose, but rather their capacity to pick, choose, combine an consume a wide gamut of the social strata. The 'highbrow snob' is almost dead. In its place is a cosmopolitan elite that freely consumes high an low culture, and everything in between. The new adolescent elite listen to classical and rap; they eat at fin restaurants and at diners. They are at ease everywhere in the world." (Khan 2011:151). Like Kahn's adolescent elites, the new female cosmopolitan elites that attend WIN listen to opera and participate in African drumming. WIN teaches them to feel increasingly at ease in the global world in which they live, move and operate. Part of the way global elites and their institutions appear then to be more multicultural, diverse and open, is to look less like the old boys clubs of yesteryear and more like a microcosm of our diverse social worlds.

WIN DAY THREE: *GROWING AS AGENTS OF POSSIBILITY*

A significant number of the women who participate in WIN conferences are both attendees and presenters (as I was that year). They are themselves, as we shall see, active agents in the production of a new elite feminine and increasingly multi-cultural affective climate. The plenary session–entitled *Growing as Agents of Possibility*–took place on the third and final day of the conference. During the session, I sat with three other participants on stage in large, comfortable white chairs. The set reminded me of a talk-show set on television. Soon, Kirsten the creator and organizer of WIN introduced the theme of the panel and the four speakers. I gave the first presentation, a talk about my older work on Wall Street women and my present work on WHEELS, a new female mechanic collective in Brooklyn. Looking out at the audience of nearly 700 women, I felt like an outlier on the panel trying to explain, in relatively lay terms, how the culture of business shapes and constrains working women's agency.

Faith Adele, the other academic on the panel was next up. For her presentation, Faith gave an abbreviated narrative about her life–living in West African and Southeast Asia, and travelling, writing and being an activist "from Bali to Switzerland to Ghana." She told us about growing up with a Nordic-American single mother, then travelling to Nigeria as an adult to find her father and siblings, to eventually becoming Thailand's first black Buddhist nun. From my partial view of the audience, I could see that many of the women were listening raptly to her life story.

Geraldine Brown, a British woman and Managing Director of her own consulting business–Domino Perspectives–was the next to speak. She told us about being an Interfaith Minister and spiritual counsellor since her ordination in 1988 and being awarded a Postgraduate Certificate in Spiritual Development and Facilitation from the University of Surrey in 2007. Her power-point presentation focused on spirituality as being the next form of business. Her website describes a range of services she provides from consulting to performing ceremonies.

The last person to speak was Louise Mita, a native from Hawaii and President and CEO of her own business: The Art of Energy, Inc. Louisa is a certified practitioner of Chinese Energetic Medicine, Tai Chi, Qigong and Feng Shui. According to her bio on her website, she has studied metaphysical alchemy, the healing and martial arts since 1968. She has lectured and taught internationally, working with such notable organizations as the World Economic Forum. Unlike the rest of us, Louise did not give a formal power-point. Instead, much to my surprise and soon chagrin, she called Faith and myself up to stand with her on stage. She asked each of us to raise her arm and think of someone we liked a great deal. Then, she tried to push our arms downward to our sides, but we were both able to successfully match her strength. Next she asked us each to think of someone we did not like. And, surprise–with what appeared to be a light flick of the wrist, Louise was able to force each of our arms back down to our sides. The staying up and pushing down of our arms continued. Louise asked the audience to think and send positive energy our way and our arms remained up. As soon as they thought purportedly dark thoughts, our arms were back down. Over time, Louise was able to whip the audience members into a near frenzy. I felt more like I was on a Las Vegas night club with a magician on stage than anything else. Needless to say I was very glad when I finally sat back down in my seat.

What are we to make of Louise, Faith and Geraldine's life stories and their respective presentations? In part, they and their spiritual practices belong to what anthropologists Jean and John Camaroff call "messianic, millennial capitalism: a capitalism that presents itself as a gospel of salvation; a capitalism that if rightly harnessed is invested with the capacity wholly to transform the universe of the marginalized and disempowered" (Comaroff and Comaroff 1999 cited in 2000). Thus, for example, Louise would have us believe that simply thinking positive thoughts will provide WIN participants with the capacity to be positive, successful business people. Producing wealth here does not depend upon the traditional physical labour of work, but rather the labouring of and on the body itself.

Recently, feminist anthropologist Carol Freeman in her ethnography – *Entrepreneurial Selves: Neoliberal Respectability* and *the Making of a Caribbean Middle Class* (Freeman 2014) – observes a growing dimension of entrepreneurialism and new middle-class subjectivities in contemporary Barbados that she sees as "intimately connected to the changing neoliberal landscape–a growing appeal of new forms of spiritual practices and belonging, including" ... "a flourishing marketplace of self-help, counseling, bodily treatments and what might be broadly understood as an incipient 'therapeutic culture'" (Illouz 2008 cited in Freeman 2014: 169). In several cases, she notes that "entrepreneurs reshaped the nature of their businesses in line with the kinds of struggles they themselves were experiencing" (Freeman 2014: 174). WIN panellists, Faith, Geraldine and Louise, are similar cases in point. In their biographies on and off line, they discuss the ways their personal journeys led them to introspection and eventually new lines of work in the spiritual and healing fields. Modes of therapy and self-care have become a means for financial enterprise and new professional middle-class subjectivities, subjectivities that the literature on white corporate feminism has, at this point in time, paid little if any attention.

CONCLUSION: FEMINISMS AS ASSEMBLAGES

To conclude, I want to return to recent work on whether and to what extent elites and their institutions have mainstreamed, weeded out or co-opted the radical politics of 1960s and 1970s feminism. I have argued that by positing a singular causality (neoliberal capitalism) or a special category of actors (white female elites) such universal principles tend to view different sites of "neoliberal feminism" as instantiations of a singular economic system. However, as I have tried to show, we should account for the historical complexity and cultural specificity of these particular engagements rather than subject them to economic reductionism (Newman 2012).

Moreover, the argument that elites have co-opted feminism leaves virtually no room for complexity, ambiguity or resistance. But as Newman contends, there is no singular neoliberal capitalism or feminism. How then is this multiplicity to be understood? If we think of global elite feminisms as assemblages, then we can see them instead as multiple, mobile and connective (Newman 2012). People, stories, and things do not move in a uniform fashion from what was once called the "East" or "Third World" to the "West" or from "black feminist" practice to "corporate white feminist" practice. Rather, when feminist and other kinds of projects encounter each other, rather than the former erasing the other, participants *selectively* appropriate aspects of them into novel configurations and take them to new places (Newman 2012: 163).

For example, when women come together at conferences like WIN they participate in at least two main circuits. The first consists of women executive-types on the global corporate conference circuit; the other is composed of the gurus and artists like the drummers. Both sets of participants are literally moving in and out of a variety of spaces and encounters. Moreover, individual actors are also moving within their own circuitries. So, for example, Faith Adele, the black female-identified travel priestess performs at corporate conferences, plus she also is deeply imbricated in a circuit of travel writers, specifically black feminist travel writers. It is in delving into her biography, as well tracing her movements that we can begin to consider how white feminists and their feminism do not necessarily always appropriate everyone and everything (Fisher Forthcoming).

Indeed, I believe that we are witnessing glimmers of the fall of the hegemony of global white elite feminism, at least a certain form. Recently, for example, Anne Marie-Slaughter, the President and CEO of The New America Foundation, and author of several controversial articles on corporate women's work-family balance, published a new book: *Unfinished Business* (2015). In her book, Slaughter calls out "plutocratic feminism," and argues for its replacement by intersectional feminism, a feminism that emphasizes the intersections of gender, race, class and other forms of different (see Bloom 2015). This move represents a new growing trend amongst white corporate feminist leaders and their networks. Indeed, for the past several years, an emerging black feminist intelligentsia has made its presence known in on- and offline. Faith Adele and others, in the wake of the rise of social media and more recently the Black Women's and Girls Lives Matter movement are challenging white elite feminist ideas and practices–by writing blogs critiquing white feminism; attending global conferences; and continuing to create their own workshops on black feminist spirituality and self-care. But all this, including their impact on white corporate feminist spirituality, remains to be ethnographically followed through and theoretically developed in terms of ideas and understanding (Fisher Forthcoming).

NOTE

1. Kirstin's words are based on field notes I took during the 2014 conference. WIN Leaders and participants may disagree with some of their interpretations of their words and experiences here, but I have tried to capture the complexities, ambiguities and anxieties of their world.

REFERENCES

Aschoff, Nicole. 2015. *The New Prophets of Capital.* New York: Verso Books.

Aspers, Patrik, and Asaf Darr. 2011. "Trade Shows and the Creation of Market and Industry." *The Sociological Review* 59(4): 758–778.

Bloom, Ester. 2015. "The Rise and Fall of Plutocrat Feminism." *The Atlantic Magazine*, November 3.

Comaroff, Jean, and John Comaroff. 2000. "Millennial Capitalism: First Thoughts on a Second Coming." *Public Culture* 12(2) (2000): 291–343.

Crowley, Karlyn. 2011. *Feminisms New Age: Gender, Appropriation, and the Afterlife of Essentialism*. Albany, NY: Suny Press.

Davies, William. 2015. *The Happiness Industry: How the Government and Big Business Sold Us Well-Being*. New York: Verso Books.

Eisenstein, Hester. 2009. *Feminism Seduced: How Global Elites Use Women's Labor and Ideas to Exploit the World*. Boulder, CO: Paradigm.

Elliot, Anthony, and John Urry. 2010. *Mobile Lives*. New York: Routledge Press.

Fisher, Melissa. 2006. "Navigating Wall Street Women's Gendered Networks in the New Economy." In *Frontiers of Capital: Ethnographic Reflections on the New Economy*, eds. M. Fisher and G. Downey. Durham, NC: Duke University Press.

Fisher, Melissa. 2010. "Wall Street Women: Engendering Global Finance in the Manhattan Landscape." *City and Society: The Journal for the Society for Urban, National, and Transnational/Global Anthropology* 22(2): 262–285.

Fisher, Melissa. 2012. *Wall Street Women*. Durham: Duke University Press.

Fisher, Melissa. 2015. "Wall Street Women: Professional Saviors of the Global Economy." *Critical Perspectives on International Business* 11(2): 137–155.

Fisher, Melissa. Forthcoming. *White Corporate Feminism and Its Discontents*: Manuscript in progress.

Fraser, Nancy. 2009. "Feminism, Capitalism and the Cunning of History." *New Left Review* 56: 97–117.

Freeman, Carla. 2013. *Entrepreneurial Selves: Neoliberal Respectability and the Making of a Caribbean Middle Class*. Durham and London: Duke University Press.

Freeman, Carla. 2014. *Entrepreneurial Selves: Neoliberal Respectability and the Making of a Caribbean Middle Class*. Durham, NC: Duke University Press.

Garsten, Christina, and Anette Nyqvist. 2013. "Entries: Engaging Organizational Worlds." In *Organizational Anthropology: Doing Ethnography in and Among Complex Organizations*, eds. C. Garsten and A. Nyqvist. London: Pluto Press.

Goldshmidt-Salamon, Karin Lisa. 2005. "Possessed by Enterprise Values & Value Creation in Mandrake Management." In *Magic, Culture & the New Economy*, eds. O. Löfgren and R. Willim. Oxford: Berg.

Harvey, David. 2005. *A Brief History of Neoliberalism*. Oxford: Oxford University Press.

Heelas, Paul. 2002. "Work ethics, soft capitalism and the turn to life." In *Cultural Economy: Cultural Analysis and Commercial Life*, eds. P. du Gay and M. Pryke. Sage: London, 78–96.

Ho, Karen. 2009. *Liquidated: An Ethnography of Wall Street*. Durham, NC: Duke University Press.

Holmes, Douglas. 2013. *Economy of Words: Communicative Imperatives in Central Banks*. Chicago: University of Chicago Press.

Jansson, Andre. 2016. "Mobile Elites: Understanding the Ambigous Lifeworlds of Sojourners, Dwellers and Homecomers." *European Journal of Cultural Studies* 19(5): 421–434.

Kahn, Shamus. 2011. *Privilege: The Making of an Adolescent Elite at St. Paul's School.* Princeton, NJ: Princeton University Press.

Kahn, Shamus Rahman. 2012. *Privilege: The Making of an Adolescent Elite at St. Paul's School.* Princeton: Princeton University Press.

Kantola, Johanna, and Judith Squires. 2012. "From State Feminism to Market Feminism." *International Political Science Review* 33(4): 382–400.

Lind, Michael. 1995. *The Next American Nation: The New Nationalism and the Fourth American Revolution.* New York: Routledge.

Lipsitz, George. 2011. *How Racism Takes Place.* Philadelphia, PA: Temple University Press.

Martin, Randy. 2002. *Financialization of Everyday Life.* Philadelphia, PA: Temple University Press.

McGee, Micki. 2007. *Self Help, Inc.: Makeover Culture in American Life.* Oxford: Oxford University Press.

McKenna, Steve, M.N. Ravishankar, and David Weir. 2015. "Critical Perspectives on the Globally Mobile Professional and Managerial Class." *Critical Perspectives on International Business* 11(2): 118–121.

McRobbie, Angela. 2009. *The Aftermath of Feminism: Gender, Culture and Social Change.* London: Sage Publications.

Moreton, Bethany. 2007. "The Soul of Neoliberalism." *Social Text* 25(392): 103–123.

Newman, Janet. 2012. *Working the Spaces of Power: Activism, Neoliberalism and Gendered Labor.* London: Bloomsbury Academic.

Ortner, Sherry. 2011. "On Neoliberalism." *Anthropology of This Century.* Issue 1, May 2011, London.

Ramos-Zayas. 2012. *Street Therapists: Race, Affect, and Neoliberal Personhood in Latino Newark.* Chicago: University of Chicago Press.

Roberts, Adrienne. 2012. Financial Crisis, Financial Firms…and Financial Feminism? The Rise of 'Transnational Business Feminism' and the Necessity of Marxist-Feminist IPE. *Socialist Studies / Études socialistes: The Journal of the Society for Socialist Studies / Revue de la Société d'études socialistes.*

Rothkopf, David. 2008. *The Superclass: The Global Power Elite and the World They Are Making.* New York: Farrar, Straus and Giroux.

Rottenberg, Catherine. 2014. "Happiness and the Liberal Imagination: How Superwoman Became Balanced." *Feminist Studies* 40(1): 144–168.

Roy, Nilanjana. 2013. "'Davos for Women' May Marginalize Female Leaders." *Time Magazine, Business & Tech*, June 8.

Sandberg, Sheryl. 2013. *Lean in: Women, Work and the Will to Lead.* New York: Knopf.

Sanders, Jen, and Renita Thedvall (eds.). 2017. *Meeting Ethnography. Meetings as Key Technologies of Contemporary Governance, Development, and Resistance.* New York: Routledge Studies in Anthropology series.

Sherman, Rachel. 2007. *Class Acts: Service and Inequality in Luxury Hotels.* Berkeley, CA: University of California Press.

Slaughter, Anne-Marie. 2015. *Unfinished Business: Women, Men, Work, Family.* New York City: Random House.

Sörbom, Adrienne, and Christina Garsten. 2015. Consequences of a Liquid Mandate: World Economic Forum and the Partial Organizing of Global Agendas. Paper presented at The 31st EGOS Colloquium 2015.

Traube, Elizabeth. 1992. *Dreaming Identities: Class, Gender, and Generation in Hollywood Movies.* Boulder, CO: Westview Press.

Valenti, Jessica. 2014. "The Empowerment Elite Claims Feminism." *The Nation,* March 3.

Wright, Mills. C. 1956. *The Power Elite.* New York: Oxford University Press.

Zaloom, Caitlin. 2006. *Out of the Pits: Traders and Technology From Chicago to.* London. Chicago: University of Chicago Press.

URL

URL: http://www.eomega.org: https://www.eomega.org/omega-in-action/key-initiatives/omega-womens-leadership-center http://www.emerging women.org: http://www.emergingwomen.com

The Therapeutic Square: The Psychotherapy Fair from an Anthropological Perspective

Hans Tunestad

INTRODUCTION: THE PSYCHOTHERAPEUTIC ARENA

"Do you know what you should write a book about?" he said. "You should write about the two cultures in psychiatry–that is, the scientific and humanistic, the medical and the psychotherapeutic."

"Perhaps I should," I responded. "However, there is already such a book. It is called *Of Two Minds* and written by an anthropologist named Tanya Luhrmann."

He gasped. His eyes were wide open. The whites of his eyes suddenly appeared to have a red shade to them. He stared at me like I had said something shocking. And perhaps, to him, it was. Then he urged me to repeat the title and the name of the author, and immediately wrote it down.

We sat at the crowded café in the main hall at the Psychotherapy Fair, a gathering that takes place every second year in Stockholm, Sweden. The man I was talking to was a new acquaintance. He had sat down at my table, simply because there was hardly anywhere else to sit. I introduced

H. Tunestad (✉)
Department of Social Anthropology, Stockholm University,
Stockholm, Sweden

© The Author(s) 2017
H. Høyer Leivestad, A. Nyqvist (eds.), *Ethnographies of Conferences and Trade Fairs*, DOI 10.1007/978-3-319-53097-0_4

myself, told him that I was doing fieldwork for my doctoral thesis in anthropology, and we started talking. He said that he had come to the fair to learn more about interesting developments within psychotherapy, to get updated on what was going on in the business, so to speak. He mentioned a seminar about EMDR, a type of therapy I had to admit I knew absolutely nothing about. He explained that it stood for Eye Movement Desensitization and Reprocessing, and tried to explain how the therapist moves a pencil in front of the patient's eyes in order to–well, I was already lost. He then changed subject and started talking about anthropology. It turned out that he had actually studied anthropology many years ago. And that was when he boldly suggested what I should write a book about.

This chapter, then, is about the Psychotherapy Fair. For those who want to be informed on psychotherapy today, as it appears in a Swedish context, the fair is probably a good place to start. A great variety of projects are presented at a number of seminars and at the exhibitions in the main hall. Research groups from scientific institutions, or from different psychiatric or psychotherapeutic clinics, present their results. There are presentations of newly published books. Different psychotherapeutic associations present their ideas and work. Public and private health care organizations employing psychotherapists inform about their psychotherapeutic activities. Counsellors and psychologists working at schools or companies or other kinds of organizations present their work. One finds a host of different psychodynamic, humanistic, cognitive, behavioural, cognitive behavioural and other approaches represented–in short, a wide variety of psychotherapeutic projects and approaches put to work in every facet of human life from birth to death.

One of the main characteristics of the Psychotherapy Fair, then, is its diversity. Yet another distinguishing characteristic of the Fair is its function as a common ground; it is a place to propagate different types of psychological treatment. This was perhaps the reason for my new friend's gasping when I mentioned *Of Two Minds*. The book confirmed his identification as a psychotherapist–that is, in opposition to the doctors, the psychiatrists, and well in line with the common ground at the Fair. At the Psychotherapy Fair we thus find a diversification within an overarching framework. Questions about what different approaches have in common, what sets them apart, the possibilities for integration of approaches, and similar issues, are constantly discussed at the Fair.

Put simply, there are two main emic distinctions within the psychotherapeutic arena in Sweden today. The first distinction is between psychotherapists with a state authorization on the one hand and therapists with other types of certifications, such as coaches, counsellors, and others (and occasionally with no certification at all) on the other. The second distinction is between psychodynamic and cognitive behavioural approaches (which also both have their respective subdivisions). Moreover, these two dominant approaches are both opposed to other approaches that do not readily fit into either of the two categories. This makes up a complex pattern of partly overlapping segmentary oppositions (cf. Evans-Pritchard 1968). In other words, it is not so easy to determine exactly what constitutes a "professional" or an "industry" in the case of contemporary Swedish psychotherapy.

In relation to the more general aim of this book–to understand how professionals are created and industries shaped in and through field-configuring events such as conferences and trade fairs–the Psychotherapy Fair is thus a case that is far from self-evident. I here argue that the Psychotherapy Fair constitutes a case that, by indirectly problematizing notions such as "professional" and "industry," offers a specific perspective on how large-scale professional gatherings, professionalization and industrialization are related to each other and thus may enhance our understanding of all three phenomena. In order to accomplish such an understanding I will first outline the diversities and commonalities of the "psychotherapeutic" as it appears at the Psychotherapy Fair, and then situate the ethnographic field in the wider societal context of the new world of work in the present phase of industrialization. First of all, however, some theoretical and methodological considerations are necessary.

SITUATING THE FAIR AS A FIELD

Doing fieldwork at the fair is not unproblematic, since the event has the duration of merely two to three days and takes place every second year, thus offering no possibility for long-term participant observation. It is therefore somewhat of a challenge to accomplish a "thick," rather than merely a "thin," description (Geertz 1973) of the fair. Other investigations into large-scale professional gatherings have met this challenge by either taking into account a number of different fairs or festivals or by applying a historical or at least longitudinal perspective, thus widening the field beyond the single event, and through this opening up for more interpretative depth (see e.g. Aspers and Darr 2011; Moeran and Pedersen 2011). In line with the latter perspective, I here argue that the Psychotherapy Fair can be a very productive site to do ethnographic fieldwork if such fieldwork is of a transtemporal character (Ullberg 2013), as well as situated in a wider societal context through complementary media, historical and archival studies (cf. Gusterson 1997; Thomas 1991). I will here situate the Psychotherapy Fair within the most recent phase of industrial development, that is, within what Boltanski and Chiapello (2005) call the "new spirit of capitalism." The question in relation to this point of view, then, is if, and how, contemporary psychotherapy is consonant with the present phase of industrialization.

In *The New Spirit of Capitalism* (2005) Boltanski and Chiapello provide a complex view of the capitalist system, opening up a perspective where internal change as a response to external critique is a part of the system itself. The so-called new spirit of capitalism emerged when the capitalist system tried to readjust itself in response to the leftist critique of the 1960s which stressed the need for liberation from inauthenticity, that is, the need to get beyond alienation. Put simply, Boltanski and Chiapello argue that the capitalist system from the 1970s onwards absorbed this critique. Managerial thought and practice started stressing autonomy and self-governance as important values to promote in the workplace. This also meant refashioning itself into more of a network character, an organizational form that allegedly frees people from the dehumanizing constraints of the bureaucratic "machines" that organizations largely constituted during the much of the twentieth century. Career opportunities are in this networked world replaced by a succession of projects, in the end making everyone his or her own ultimate project (see Boltanski and Chiapello 2005: 84, 97–98, 110–111).

I will here argue that at the Psychotherapy Fair psychological treatment emerges as a therapeutic counterpart of contemporary management ideals and practices. New therapies are today often set up as a kind of guided self-help, where the patients are supposed to take an active part in their own treatment. And to the extent that the patients are successfully cured, they come out of the therapy with an enhanced capability for interaction and self-management, and thus the competence to take personal responsibility for both their own work and health. These responsibilities are in effect two sides of the same coin; what constitutes the ideal patient today is also what constitutes the ideal worker.

This also means that psychotherapeutic knowledge is not only useful in healing patients with psychiatric diagnoses. And the Psychotherapy Fair, accordingly, not only displays psychotherapy in the strict sense of the term, but also examples of how a psychotherapeutic way of thinking and acting is used in a number of spheres outside of health care in Sweden today. If defining anthropology in line with Hannerz (1992) as "the social organization of meaning," then the Fair is an event where this organizing of meaning becomes evident when it comes to the psychotherapeutic field in Sweden more generally. The Psychotherapy Fair then emerges, if twisting Schwartzman (1989) just a little bit, as this organization "writ small." In other words, the Psychotherapy Fair is a condensed version not just of contemporary Swedish psychotherapy, but also of the "psychotherapeutic" in Sweden today.

In order to capture this contemporary "psychotherapeutic" I conducted transtemporal fieldwork encompassing the Psychotherapy Fairs in 2004, 2006, 2008 and again 2014, though most intensively in 2004 and 2006. As is probably often the case when researching conferences, trade fairs and meetings, so-called participant observation was to a large degree a question of "engaged listening" (Forsey 2010: 560), that is, not only or even mainly observing, but also listening deeply by making use of an "ethnographic imaginary" (2010: 567) to uncover the meaningful patterns in the talks in which I took part. This was crucial, for example, during participation in different seminars, in discussions with participants, in some interviews made before or after the fair itself, and elsewhere. It is now time to look more closely at what this fieldwork amounted to.

A DIVERSITY OF THERAPY

The Psychotherapy Fair has been held biennially since 2000. In 2000 and 2002 it was held in central Stockholm. From 2004 to 2008 it was held at *Stockholmsmässan*, a large exhibition complex in a suburb of Stockholm called Älvsjö. In 2010 and 2012 it moved back to central Stockholm, and once again relocated to *Stockholmsmässan* in Älvsjö in 2014 and onwards. According to the program of the third fair in 2004:

> this fair is unique in Sweden, as well as in the rest of the world. Exhibitors are licensed psychotherapists, their organizations, workplaces, and institutions. Specially invited participants are patient organizations, affected unions, publishing companies, politicians, researchers, and others that work to promote mental health, psychotherapy, and psychological counselling.... In about 100 showcases and at about 270 seminars/lectures, mini-lectures

at a speaker's corner and panel discussions the visitors are given rich possibilities to take part of, and discuss, the wide field of licensed psychotherapists, such as work with patients/clients in medical treatment, health care, and rehabilitation and pre-emptive work, and work in corporate health care, schools, and education, research and development.[1]

In 2006 the program stated that the fair had "become a forum for information, knowledge dissemination, developing discussions and informal gatherings for everyone who is active within and interested in the diversified field of psychotherapy and psychology." At the time this obviously meant some seminars, showcases, books and leaflets were not really about psychotherapy in the strict sense of the term at all. In the program for 2016 it was stated that the fair was "the meeting place for qualified psychotherapeutic work," and participants were encouraged to put together their "own conference program."

The Psychotherapy Fair has, thus, fluctuated somewhat in both scope and content. During the early 2000s it was more open, inviting the general public to a larger extent, with an average of around 2000 visitors (with a peak in 2002 of around 3000 visitors). From 2012 on the number of visitors was roughly half that, and though the fair still had some seminars directed to the general public, it had become more like a conference where therapists with different backgrounds and following different approaches could get together and take part of a diversity of therapeutic work and discuss common issues.[2]

So the Psychotherapy Fair is in many ways like a scientific conference in that people go there to keep up with what is happening in the field of knowledge they are a part of, and to learn about different institutions and organizations and what they are doing. To a certain extent it also resembles an industrial fair or trade fair in that it exhibits items that are for sale, such as books or newly developed treatment programs, or for that matter books that constitute newly developed treatment programs. The fair thus resembles a sort of public square, both in the sense of being a place where you may encounter and chat with other people and gain new ideas, and in the sense of being a marketplace. It could therefore be said to make up something of a "therapeutic square," and even more so since the exchange in both cases is related to therapeutic matters. Because what remains consistent at the Psychotherapy Fair is the character it has as a meeting place for those interested in, as the 2006 program stated, the "diversified field of psychotherapy."

ENTERING THE FAIR

Let us now enter the Fair. It basically has two parts: seminars and exhibitions. After paying the fee, getting your nametag and program, as well as the tickets for the seminars of your choice, the natural way to approach the fair is to proceed into the exhibition hall. Here people wander around and look at the showcases–during the 2000s usually about one hundred of them–occasionally stopping and chatting with an exhibitor or other visitors. Here you also find a few more or less crowded cafés where you can sit down for a break and a chance to contemplate the seminars, or perhaps chat about them with colleagues or other visitors. If the fair, figuratively speaking, constitutes a sort of therapeutic square, then the main hall actually gives the impression of a public square or marketplace, and no less so at the fairs when it has been situated in one of the larger halls at *Stockholmsmässan*, where the huge rectangular room with its high ceiling almost gives it an outdoor sense.

In the exhibition hall there are personnel and showcases from professional associations, from organizations employing psychologists and psychotherapists, both public and private, and from different academies. A specific kind of showcases is the type set up by publishing houses. Some are small, specialized, sometimes even just marketing a single work, whereas the larger publishers are selling a wide variety of books spanning from theoretical and methodological works to self-help manuals, and from neuroscience to social psychology. At the fair you not only find well-known approaches represented such as cognitive therapy, behaviour therapy, cognitive behaviour therapy, psychoanalysis and different psychodynamic approaches, but also (publicly) less well-known therapies such as hypnotherapy, art therapy, dance therapy, music therapy, Eye Movement Desensitization and Reprocessing (EMDR) and Imago, just to mention a few. There are also a variety of mini-seminars taking place in this hall that altogether treat a similar width of subjects as the showcases.

The seminars show even more diversity than what can be found in the exhibition hall. In addition to the aforementioned subjects, I also noticed, just to take a few examples, seminars dealing with the theories and practices related to the idea of emotional intelligence as applied in some Swedish schools, seminars describing research done to produce methods for the healing of stress-related illnesses, seminars dealing with organizational consultancy work, and with supervision in schools. Important are also the panel discussions where therapists from different "schools" meet and discuss, sometimes debate, common concerns. These could be about psychotherapy integration, the similarities between different approaches, the efficacy of different treatments, and similar topics. The by far most crowded seminar I took part in was a presentation of a new book by well-known neuroscientist Antonio Damasio.

When it comes to the size of the seminars there is a significant diversity as well. Some seminars take place in the huge lecture hall with room for several hundred people, some in smaller lecture halls, some in seminar rooms for about forty people, and some in small seminar rooms for sometimes just eight to ten people. In any case, the lively atmosphere of the exhibition hall all melts away once you enter a seminar. In most cases a solemn atmosphere reigns: a lecturer delivers a speech to a thoughtful audience. In the lecture halls the atmosphere even appears to have been consciously densified with dark blue tapestries, softened lights, and a cool breeze from the air-conditioning. Here people walk slowly and carefully between the rows of chairs so as not to make some noise, even talking with a soft voice.

The fair has two types of passes, one that grants admittance to the main hall with all the showcases and mini-seminars, as well as some of the other seminars, and one that grants full access to all the seminars offered. The latter are mainly for the professionals, though not only psychotherapists or psychologists visit these seminars, but also social workers, teachers, journalists and occasionally an anthropologist. This variety becomes evident for example at some seminars, held in small seminar rooms, where the chairs are occasionally arranged in the form of a horseshoe and the participants are expected to introduce themselves.

The first time I visited such a seminar I felt I had come to both the best and the worst place possible: the worst since this demand for self-presentation unleashed a paralyzing wave of anxiety within me (when struck by the very awkward thought that the others would most certainly see me as an intruder), but the best place since I suddenly realized I probably needed psychotherapy. However, when I heard the others presenting themselves, some mentioning occupations such as teacher and social worker–obviously they were not all psychotherapists–I understood that perhaps I was not such an odd figure in this context as I had thought. I then remembered the words I had heard at some management courses I had participated in as a part of my fieldwork for my doctoral thesis, where the importance of personal development for efficient interaction had been stressed. That sounded therapeutic enough. So when it was my turn to introduce myself I simply stated that I was an anthropologist involved in a research project that was at least partly about how efficiency and personal development can be joined together. I had hardly shut my mouth before one of the speakers pointed her finger at me, smiled, and said: "That's right! That's right!" She then wrote my words on the whiteboard and said that it is not only about personal development, but also about health. "And," her colleague added, "well-being!" Quite contrary to my initial apprehension, I realized I was suddenly in.

As is evident here, not only was the presence of an anthropologist as such at one of these seminars apparently insignificant, but the words of an anthropologist–quoting the words of some management consultants– could even be both interesting and useful at a seminar dealing with psychotherapeutic matters. Psychotherapy was obviously something not only for, or even of, psychotherapists. This indeterminate quality of contemporary Swedish psychotherapy reflects the dual character of the psychotherapeutic "industry"–that is, as embracing both a profession with a state authorization and being something of a more general approach to how to conduct one's life.

To sum up, the Psychotherapy Fair involves a variety of participants taking part in a variety of activities concerning a variety of subjects occurring simultaneously in a variety of rooms. The Psychotherapy Fair is a complex information-dense large-scale gathering for professionals and interested laypersons knit together by the constant focus on psychological treatment and related issues. Especially for lay people, perhaps being presumptive patients interested in some kind of treatment, but to a certain extent for professionals as well, looking for anything from basic ideas to methods to pre-packaged programs that are for sale, the diversity of the field gives it an almost playful and consumption-like character, with a variety of opportunities to, so to speak, shop around–and where it is ultimately up to each and every individual to decide what he or she considers useful (cf. Dumit 2001). It all makes up, in other words, a psychotherapeutic square.

Work, Work, Work

If the content of the fair is indeed characterized by the diversified field of psychotherapy, its temporality keeps it more cohesive. The Psychotherapy Fair has a pulse of its own, created by people moving about. It has a tight schedule, where the seminars follow one after the other, with just short coffee breaks and lunch in between. The crowd thus moves into the seminar rooms on schedule, and out of the seminar rooms and into the exhibition hall, and out of the exhibition hall and again into the seminar rooms on schedule, at lunch time a stream of people move across the bridge over the railway into the small centre of Älvsjö where a number of restaurants are situated, and then back again when the lunch break is over, and then into the seminar rooms, and then out of the seminar rooms. At least when it comes to the pulse, the Psychotherapy Fair has something of a mid-twentieth century industrial-era factory to it.

That psychotherapy today is intimately related to work life is even more evident at some seminars, both regarding the composition of the therapies presented and the wider societal transformations these therapies are part of. To give the impression of what the seminars are like I will here give an example from a seminar that dealt with the treatment of patients suffering from "exhaustion syndrome," at the time a newly created diagnosis that was intended to replace the diagnosis of burnout in Sweden. The diagnosis was later included in the ICD-10-SE, the Swedish version of ICD-10, the tenth revision of the WHO's International Statistical Classification of Diseases and Related Health Problems.[3] The aim of the project was to produce a marketable program for the rehabilitation of patients suffering from this condition.

So, imagine yourself in a seminar room with close to forty other people. The speaker presents himself as a psychiatrist and psychotherapist who has been part of the development of this project–and then releases a continuous flow of PowerPoint slides. Put briefly, you are told that this is a project worked out for primary care, not specialist care. It is not really about psychotherapy, in the strict sense of the term, but about therapy given by "experienced caretakers," such as nurses, counsellors or social workers. These "experienced caretakers" are given a brief psychotherapeutic education, so that they, in turn, may assist the patients in coming to terms with their problems.

The project is described as mainly consisting of a "cognitive discussion group" with eight participants, a series of fourteen sessions where each session has a specified content, and with the aim of creating a dynamic in the group that will give extra value, so to speak, beyond what a dyadic patient-therapist relationship can give. The themes of the sessions include affect theory, cognitive theory, methods for strengthening one's self-esteem, coping and other topics. The sessions generally follow the same pattern, beginning with a breathing exercise, which is followed by a recapitulation of the last meeting. Then the participants discuss their homework and other issues they feel are important. The group leader then lectures on the theme of the session, which is reflected on, where after the participants construct their own home work until the next session, and then the session ends, just as it started, with a breathing exercise. Through the therapeutic process the participants are supposed to achieve a deeper understanding of themselves and in the end work out so-called coping strategies–that is, well-functioning ways of handling themselves.

These patients, you are told, often have a long history in health care before they receive therapy, through which they have learnt to be victims. What they need is more self-esteem, in order to get away from the role of victim and instead become actors. Yet this problem is challenging, the speaker asserts, since standard solutions do not apply here. Traditional medicine is here too much like fixing a car: you think you have the solution and then "fix" the patient. But this is not a problem that any doctor easily can fix. It is about helping the patient lead a better life; to help the patient get away from the role of victim, and on to being an actor taking care of him- or herself. The latter is especially important since a relapse is common among these patients. When they get out of the therapy they should have the tools they need to stay healthy.

At the end of the seminar a person in the audience asks if she could get the manual for the program. The speaker first answers "no," but then hesitates when asked to explain why. He then suddenly says, "Well, okay, this is not a scientific conference, it is a commercial fair, everyone is into marketing," and he urges those interested to buy the course in order to become coaches in this program (thus implying that this was the way to get the manual). On a question about verification or evidence for the efficacy of the treatment, he answers that the goal of the therapy is to diminish sick leave among participants, which has been measured in relation to both those who still remain in line for treatment and a parallel research project. Then the seminar is over and everybody leaves the room, some quickly, some more slowly.

This is a typical example of a seminar at the Psychotherapy Fair. The presentation is knowledge-dense and thus rather demanding to listen to. The content of the presentation also reveals a kind of therapy that is radically different from the kind of "talking cure" (Leahey 2004: 275–276) that Freud pioneered a hundred years earlier. Regarding all its specific features the previous described therapy is almost the opposite of classical psychoanalysis. We do not find a dyadic and hierarchically organized therapy, based on a theoretically refined drive theory, where a physician administers a time-consuming cure to a wealthy neurotic housewife (to be). Instead we here find a time-limited treatment–based on a mixture of theoretical models all worked out during the post-war years, such as cognitive psychology, affect theory and group dynamics–directed at the rehabilitation of a group of employees so they can go back to work, mainly by aiding these employees in working out their own conscious strategies for how to manage their lives. In brief, psychotherapy has here come to stress the values of autonomy and authenticity, as well as responsibility and efficiency, which also frame contemporary management discourse (Boltanski and Chiapello 2005; Fleming 2009).

In this case, and several others, the presentation also has, probably for most psychotherapists and lay persons alike, an interesting content, since it is about a much discussed societal problem. Yet the character of the talk is at the same time plain, not to say unremarkable–the audience sits in silence (though occasionally humming, or clearing their throats, stretching their backs, scratching their necks, then taking some notes) and listens to the speaker talking, in a more or less monotonous voice, while one PowerPoint slide after the other floats by. The temporal character of the Psychotherapy Fair is thus not the "carnival time" of the fairs and festivals in the creative industries (Moeran and Pedersen 2011: 6), but more often "business as usual time." That is to say, participating in an event such as the Psychotherapy Fair is more of just another day at work, reality is not turned upside down; the gathering is merely yet another project in the seemingly endless row of projects, where each and every person in the end is his or her own main project (Boltanski and Chiapello 2005).

And noticeable is that the fair has a time of its own in addition to its temporal pulse, that is, the actual temporal character of the specific event that is the Fair. The Psychotherapy Fair as a societal phenomenon also has a beginning, as well as a continuation, in time, and as such must be understood, I will here argue, as part of the transformations of the Swedish welfare state and society in recent decades.

SCIENTIZATION

What struck me as most conspicuous when I first visited the Psychotherapy Fair was the frequent use of statistics in the presentations of new treatments. Though having worked as a caretaker in a psychiatric institution several years earlier, as well as having read some of the classics such as Freud and Jung, it had never entered my mind that statistics constituted an important part of psychotherapy. However, statistics were used in a very specific way at the fair. They were not presented as a tool used in therapy, but as a way of proving the efficacy of the treatment. Psychotherapy has here adapted itself to the so-called medical model, using randomized controlled treatment trials (RCTs).[4] This has meant that to delimit, compare and evaluate, where the first is a precondition for the other two, appear as important ingredients in the development of new therapies – making it possible to measure efficacy and (partly through this) also keeping the costs of therapy low. The latter is also, as seen in the seminar described earlier, the reason for introducing psychoeducation into therapies making them into a sort of guided self-help. Through this the patients are involved in the therapeutic work, and the risk for a relapse when the actual therapy has ended is diminished.

The application of the "medical model" also means that psychotherapy has become scientific in a new way. Put simply, verifiability here means that the statistics are good. The old animosity and interschool struggle between psychoanalysis and behaviourism, including the debate over whether psychotherapy could or should be seen as a science, that supposedly characterized psychotherapy up until the 1960s (Saugstad 2001: 477) here made less sense. The panels arranged at the fair on the topic of efficacy in psychotherapy were not heated debates. Rather, they had a sort of reconciliatory spirit to them. At these panels, representatives from different approaches delivered statements about their respective ways of treating patients and clients. There were really no arguments against anything, or at least not any type of psychotherapy, launched here. All agreed that psychotherapy works, although maybe not all therapies are equally well designed to cure all types of afflictions.

It is with public management reform over the last decades (Pollit and Bouckaert 2011), that therapeutic efficiency (also implying cost-effectiveness) has become a subject of growing importance for psychotherapy (Pusch and Dobson 1994: 675; Olsson 1999). Therapies simply need to be scientifically verified in order to be funded by the public health care system. Verifiability has also, as seen in the aforementioned case, meant a movement towards manualization of therapies. Therapeutic expertise is now increasingly encoded in classifications and manuals ("pure expertises" in the words of Castel 1991: 291) and disseminated into the health care system at large, at the expense of the autonomy of physicians and other therapists, a process known as deprofessionalization (see e.g. Reeder 2006; Ritzer 2001: 185; cf.; Deleuze 1992).

In these circumstances, someone less well acquainted with the developments of psychotherapy in Sweden today (or globally for that matter) may well wonder what the place of psychoanalysis–being somewhat of the original "talking cure" (Leahey 2004: 275–276)–is in the therapeutic square of today. At the fair there are a number of presentations about psychoanalysis, or that make use of psychoanalysis. From a wider societal context, however, psychoanalysis is, at least when it comes to Sweden, being relegated to the margins of the health care apparatus. With an increasing importance of therapeutic efficiency, psychoanalysis today finds itself in an ever more hostile environment. In two major reports from The Swedish Council on Health Technology Assessment (SBU)–one about the treatment of anxiety syndromes and the other about depression–psychoanalysis is found to lack efficacy, and thus given low grades or even no grades (SBU 2004, 2005). This means that it is not recommended, or even seen as something that should be avoided in the treatment of these disorders. The same goes for the national guidelines for the treatment of these disorders published by the National Board of Health and Welfare (Socialstyrelsen 2010).

Such decisive statements hardly appeared at the Psychotherapy Fair however. At the fair there was openness towards different kinds of treatments. Psychotherapy here emerged as a number of techniques and methods that could be combined in different ways in order to treat different afflictions. Instead of interschool struggle, then, there was much talk at the fair about the integration of different approaches. It is this reconciliatory spirit that, arguably, has made the fair as a phenomenon possible. This development is also in line with the steadily increasing number of diagnoses for mental health problems, all in need of new effective therapies.

Since the common denominator for the treatments presented at the Fair is that they are all *psychological* treatments, it was another kind of therapy that appeared as the common adversary. As a participant at a seminar about therapy integration half-jokingly remarked, "Our common enemy is the 'medics' (*medicinarna*)"–by this term obviously referring to the psychiatrists. At another panel discussion the chairperson concluded that he believed that "in the future we will not talk about psychotherap*ies* (that is, in the plural), but psychological treatment," thus suggesting that if theoretical-methodological "purity" once was an issue of importance in psychotherapy, it is so no longer. Some "schools"–such as cognitive behaviour therapy, which assemble components from cognitive therapy and behaviour therapy–are already working in that direction, since they are integrative in themselves. This however, appears to be something not just concluded by university professors in panel discussions, but also agreed on by the psychotherapist in common, as described in the introductory vignette of this chapter.

POPULARIZATION

That psychotherapy–being therapy–is a part of the health care apparatus in Sweden today, as seen in the example from the seminar described earlier, is probably less surprising to most people (although far from self-evident). Yet psychotherapeutic knowledge is today also applied in work life, in schooling, and has even become a standard repertoire in the mass media– thus stretching its tentacles into the everyday life of, more or less, every citizen. Through the way these different parts of society are drawn into the Fair, it also becomes evident that the psychotherapeutic today constitutes a set of ideas and practices that binds much of present day society together.

As described before, economic considerations have in different ways become an integrated part of psychotherapy in Sweden today. Yet, this is not just a question of creating and marketing sellable therapy programs, or constantly thinking about the issue of therapeutic efficiency. Some therapists also use their knowledge about human functioning to start working with organizational efficiency as management consultants. The latter business appears to be a niche not exactly overexploited, but there are some examples. At the fair I took part in two seminars where psychotherapists described their work as management consultants in work organizations, helping out employees with personal or interactional problems and thus increasing their abilities to work. Another example was a project that dealt with a school in southern Sweden that, like many other schools, had had a problem with stress-related illness among the teachers. Through psychoeducation the personnel were given the relevant knowledge and skills to cope with their own stress reactions, thereby enhancing their functionality and reducing the overall sick leave.

Psychoeducation means giving over some of the therapeutic expertise to patients or clients in order to make them more skilled in handling themselves. At best this means that, as seen earlier, the personnel will stay healthy and well at work, since they are able to handle their own problems. From here it is just a small step to using psychoeducation as a tool for enhancing the well-being of people in general in order to help them avoid developing destructive patterns of behaviour in the first place. This is a kind of work, undertaken at some Swedish schools, that was also presented at the fair.

In the mid-2000s, psychoeducation was, however, not something that occurred only in classrooms, work organizations or closed psychotherapy sessions in Sweden. The general trend in psychotherapy towards manualization also found a favourable environment in the mass media. Since self-help manuals must be simple enough for laypersons to understand them, newspapers, television shows and other publications can represent therapeutic manuals for anyone interested. For example, at the 2008 Psychotherapy Fair a book about panic disorder called *Ingen panik* (Carlbring and Hanell 2007), meaning both "no panic" and "don't panic," was presented at a seminar. At the time of its publication this book was also described in an article in *Expressen*, one of the leading Swedish newspapers.[5] Three manuals for how to come to terms with panic attacks, all borrowed directly from the book, accompanied the article. This article was an example of the kind of therapeutic manual that could be found in the evening papers in Stockholm several times a week in the mid and late 2000s.

These examples show that psychotherapeutic theories, methods and techniques, as well as a psychotherapeutic approach in general, are made use of in diverse settings, and for a diversity of problems–stretching out well beyond what is psychotherapy in the strict sense of the term. These examples also make evident, however, that–contradictory as it may seem–within the field of psychotherapy, the increased use of guided self-help has made scientization and popularization go hand in hand.

TRANSFORMATIONS AND IDENTIFICATIONS

In Sweden, the mass mediation of psychotherapeutic theory and practice constitutes a rather novel situation. Still in the mid-1980s, there was an almost complete lack of therapeutic representations in both television and the daily press.[6] Swedish television at the time consisted of two channels guided by a public service ideology–stressing the values of objectivity, impartiality and good taste (Furhammar 2006: 20)–that aired from five in the afternoon until eleven in the evening. The daily newspapers focused on news only, publishing "hard" news. For a long time psychotherapy, in the strict sense of the term, had also been hard to get, since it was only administered by physicians to patients with a psychiatric diagnosis or to state employees with a remittance from a psychiatrist unless one wanted to pay for the whole treatment oneself (Reeder 2006: 191–195). As described before, all this was to change in the decades to come.

During much of the twentieth century in Sweden, the treatment of mental health problems had a secluded character to it. Most conspicuous was probably the treatment of the seriously mentally ill which occurred in mental hospitals located at the outskirts of the big cities or in the countryside. Here the afflicted were subjected to a strict disciplinary regime (Goffman 1961). In many ways, this followed the Taylorist production regime of the day where efficiency was believed to come from a thoroughgoing division of work following strict procedures. And until the 1970s, psychotherapy was not highly regarded within the medical establishment in Sweden, but largely labelled as unscientific (Olsson 1999: 149). There existed no state subsidized education of psychotherapists, few professional organizations and few psychotherapists.

However, in continental Europe, Great Britain and America, alternative versions of expertise in psychiatric matters were constructed during the post-war years. Most important here was probably the humanistic movement and the cognitive revolution.[7] The humanistic movement stressed the sanity and possibilities of personal growth within every individual. The cognitive revolution brought forth a perspective on humans as information handling systems–challenging the common view in psychoanalysis and behaviourism of humans as barely cultured animals–which meant that it was possible to change behavioural patterns by consciously changing thought patterns. Together with the concept of "psychoeducation" that started gaining general use during the 1980s (Bäuml et al. 2006), these developments meant that patients were increasingly seen as coworkers, competent enough to take part in their own healing processes.

This was also the direction Swedish mental health care took when the economic recession in the 1970s made new solutions necessary in the Swedish social security system. The steady increase in health care spending, which had been going on for decades, had suddenly become problematic. At the same time the public sector–of which health care was an important part–was of vital importance in the economy at large. The answer to this seemingly unsolvable problem was a compromise stressing both the responsibility of society and the responsibility of the individual. At the end of the 1970s Swedish public health discourse is reoriented in an "individualizing and totalizing" (Olsson 1999: 144) direction. Health is now to permeate all facets of life, and the individual is to take responsibility for his or her own health and public health is seen as both a public and an individual concern. In the 1980s the large mental hospitals, usually located in less populated areas, were gradually closed down and replaced by more open forms of care, which also meant that psychiatric care ceased to be something radically separated from the rest of society (Reeder 2006: 20–26, 217–219). During the following decades, psychotherapy in Sweden is gradually reoriented towards more of guided self-help (Tunestad 2014).

By the mid-2000s, psychotherapy and counselling in Sweden had lost its exclusive character and become something rather mundane. By that point there were almost 4000 licensed psychotherapists in Sweden, at least ten different professional associations, a host of diverse therapeutic approaches put to use for a growing number of mental problems (Johansson 1999: 459; *Psykoterapi* 2006; Reeder 2006: 254), and a public sphere where popular psychoeducation had become a part of the regular mass media flow. The Psychotherapy Fair can be seen as a manifestation of these developments where psychotherapy in different ways has become more of a common and public undertaking.

THE NEW SPIRIT OF THERAPEUTIC CAPITALISM

At the Psychotherapy Fair–here viewed as a condensed version of the psychotherapeutic field in Sweden–the processes of professionalization, deprofessionalization and industrialization are entwined. On the one hand, the fair is more firmly establishing psychotherapy as an important undertaking, thus strengthening the profession. On the other hand, for psychotherapists with a state authorization the fostering of a diagnostic and statistical system, and all that ensues from that such as manualization, works against their autonomy as psychotherapists. For therapists without state authorization, manualization may on the contrary actually mean a strengthening of their professional identity in the case they are licensed to follow a specific program. In a sense, even the patients are to a certain extent drawn into these processes through psychoeducation where they achieve some therapeutic autonomy and become, ideally, at least a kind of experts on themselves.

Altogether, these somewhat contradictory processes nevertheless give psychotherapy a specific direction. Much of psychotherapy today–from the professionals with a state authorization undertaking psychotherapy in the strict sense of the term, to the professionals with other types of certifications, to the more popular variants of psychological interventions found in the mass media–push psychotherapy towards a sort of life management based on a "toolbox psychology" (Tunestad 2014), that is, a guided self-help psychology based on concepts, techniques and methods almost anyone can understand and make use of by and for themselves. This has opened up for an expansion of psychotherapeutic thought and practice into a number of societal spheres, engaging diverse categories of people. Psychotherapy has through this come to have an integrative function in contemporary Swedish society. To some extent in a Durkheimian or Geertzian sense, that is, creating a common identification or culture. But perhaps even more in a Barthian sense–building bridges between what was before separated (Barth 1966).

In this expansion, the psychotherapeutic has today come to stress the same values as the "managerial"–self-regulation, responsibility, efficiency. Whether intended or not, the psychotherapeutic in contemporary Sweden shares some fundamental traits with prevalent management ideology and can thus be said to perpetuate the new spirit of capitalism. To understand contemporary Swedish psychotherapy it is therefore necessary not only to understand the present situation, or the transformations the field has gone through the last decades, but also how these changes are intimately linked to wider transformations of the welfare state and society, where not only the work of psychotherapists (and patients) has been transformed, but also the very ideals for how to organize work more generally. Contemporary managerial thought and practice stress autonomy and self-governance as important values to promote in the workplace (Boltanski and Chiapello 2005; cf. Rose 1998). This is exactly the kind of knowledge that contemporary psychotherapeutic approaches can provide. This is, therefore, as I have described elsewhere (Tunestad 2014), a society characterized by the "therapeutization of work."

Notes

1. All translations from Swedish, that is from programs, reports, journals, newspapers et cetera, are my own unless otherwise stated.
2. My description in this chapter is mainly based on the Fairs in 2004 and 2006, when I conducted the most intense field work, to some extent on the Fair in 2008, and to a lesser extent on the Fair in 2014. During the Psychotherapy Fairs in 2004, 2006 and 2008 I took part in almost thirty seminars all having a length from sixty to seventy-five minutes.

3. I will here follow Sandström (2010) and translate *utmattningssyndrom* as "exhaustion syndrome."
4. For a general discussion see Wampold and Imel (2015). For the Swedish situation, see Holmqvist and Philips (2008).
5. In a supplement called *Hallå!* (2007-09-16: 32–35).
6. The general statements about the mass media is here based on my reading of all daily newspapers in Stockholm (as well as a few union journals) in September 1987, 1997 and 2007, as well as a reading of the newspapers in the first half of September in 1977 and 1982. For a review of television see Furhammar (2006).
7. For a more exhaustive description of these developments, see Tunestad (2014).

References

Aspers, Patrik, and Asaf Darr. 2011. "Trade Shows and the Creation of Market and Industry." *The Sociological Review* 59(4): 758–778.

Barth, Fredrik. 1966. *Models of Social Organization*. London: Royal Anthropological Institute.

Bäuml, Josef, Teresa Froböse, Sibylle Kreamer, Michael Rentrop, and Pitscher-Walz Gabriele. 2006. "Psychoeducation: A Basic Psychotherapeutic Intervention for Patients with Schizophrenia and Their Families." *Schizophrenia Bulletin* 32(1): 1–9.

Boltanski, Luc, and Eve Chiapello. 2005. *The New Spirit of Capitalism*. London: Verso.

Carlbring, Per, and Åsa Hanell. 2007. *Ingen panik: Fri från panik- och ångestattacker i 10 steg med kognitiv beteendeterapi*. Stockholm: Natur och kultur.

Castel, Robert. 1991. "From Dangerousness to Risk." In *The Foucault Effect: Studies in Governmentality: With Two Lectures By and an Interview With Michel Foucault*, eds. Graham Burchell, Colin Gordon, and Peter Miller. Chicago: University of Chicago Press.

Deleuze, Gilles. 1992. "Postscript on the Societies of Control." *October* 59: 3–7.

Dumit, Joseph. 2001. "Playing Truths: Logics of Seeking and the Persistence of New Age." *Focaal* 37: 63–75.

Evans-Pritchard, Edward Evan. 1968 [1940]. *The Nuer: A Description of the Modes of Livelihood and Political Institutions of a Nilotic People*. 1st ed., repr. London: Clarendon.

Fleming, Peter. 2009. *Authenticity and the Cultural Politics of Work: New Forms of Informal Control*. Oxford: Oxford University Press.

Forsey, Martin Gerard. 2010. "Ethnography as Participant Listening." *Ethnography* 11(4): 558–572.

Furhammar, Leif. 2006. *Sex, såpor och svenska krusbär: Television i konkurrens.* Stockholm: Ekerlid.

Geertz, Clifford. 1973. *The Interpretation of Cultures.* New York: Basic Books.

Goffman, Erving. 1961. *Asylums: On the Social Situation of Mental Patients and Other Inmates.* New York: First Anchor Books.

Gusterson, Hugh. 1997. "Studying Up Revisited." *Political and Legal Anthropology Review* 20(1): 114–119.

Hannerz, Ulf. 1992. *Cultural Complexity: Studies in the Social Organization of Meaning.* New York: Columbia University Press.

Holmqvist, Rolf, and Björn Philips (eds.). 2008. *Vad är verksamt i psykoterapi?.* Stockholm: Liber.

Johansson, Per Magnus. 1999. *Freuds psykoanalys. Band II: Arvtagare i Sverige.* Göteborg: Daidalos.

Leahey, Thomas Hardy. 2004. *A History of Psychology: Main Currents in Psychological Thought.* Upper Saddle River, NJ: Pearson Prentice Hall.

Moeran, Brian, and Jesper Strandgaard Pedersen. 2011. *Negotiating Values in the Creative Industries: Fairs, Festivals and Competitive Events [Electronic resource].* Cambridge: Cambridge University Press.

Olsson, Ulf. 1999. *Drömmen om den hälsosamma medborgaren: Folkuppfostran och hälsoupplysning i folkhemmet.* Stockholm: Carlssons.

Pollit, Christopher, and Geert Bouckaert. 2011. *Public Management Reform: A Comparative Analysis – New Public Management, Governance, and the Neo-Weberian State.* Oxford: Oxford University Press.

Psykoterapi: Information om olika psykoterapiinriktningar 2006. Stockholm: Samrådsforum för psykoterapi.

Pusch, Dennis, and Keith S. Dobson. 1994. "Psychotherapy." In *Encyclopedia of Human Behaviour,* editor-in-chief V.S. Ramachandran. San Diego: Academic Press.

Reeder, Jurgen. 2006. *Psykoanalys i välfärdsstaten: Profession, kris och framtid.* Stockholm/Stehag: Brutus Östlings Bokförlag Symposion.

Ritzer, George. 2001. *Explorations in Social Theory: From Metatheorizing to Rationalization [Electronic Resource].* London: Sage.

Rose, Nikolas. 1998. *Inventing Our Selves: Psychology, Power, and Personhood.* Cambridge: Cambridge University Press.

Sandström, Agneta. 2010. *Neurocognitive and Endocrine Dysfunction in Women with Exhaustion Syndrome.* Umeå: Department of Public Health and Clinical Medicine, Departments of Radiation Sciences and Integrative Medical Biology.

Saugstad, Per. 2001. *Psykologins historia: En introduktion till dagens psykologi.* Stockholm: Bokförlaget Natur och Kultur.

SBU. 2004. *Behandling av depressionssjukdomar. En systematisk litteraturöversikt, Volym 3.* Stockholm: Statens beredning för medicinsk utvärdering (The Swedish Council on Health Technology Assessment.

SBU. 2005. *Behandling av ångestsyndrom. En systematisk litteraturöversikt, Volym 2.* Stockholm: Statens beredning för medicinsk utvärdering (The Swedish Council on Health Technology Assessment.

Schwartzman, Helen B. 1989. *The Meeting: Gatherings in Organizations and Communities.* New York: Plenum Press.

Socialstyrelsen. 2010. *Nationella riktlinjer för vård vid depression och ångestsyndrom 2010: Stöd för styrning och ledning.* Stockholm: Socialstyrelsen.

Thomas, Nicholas. 1991. "Against Ethnography." *Cultural Anthropology* 6(3): 306–322.

Tunestad, Hans. 2014. *The Therapeutization of Work: The Psychological Toolbox as Rationalization Device During the Third Industrial Revolution in Sweden.* Stockholm: Stockholm University.

Ullberg, Susann. 2013. *Watermarks: Urban Flooding and Memoryscape in Argentina.* Stockholm: Stockholm University.

Wampold, Bruce, and Zac E. Imel. 2015. *The Great Psychotherapy Debate: The Evidence for What Makes Psychotherapy Work [Electronic resource],* 2nd ed., New York: Routledge.

CHAPTER 5

Establishing the Complexity of Obesity: The Conference as a Site of Understanding Obesity as a Medical Condition

Mia Forrest

INTRODUCTION: BECOMING AN OBESITY EXPERT

Dr. Johansson, a chief physician at one of Stockholm's obesity treatment facilities, recounts the story of how she became an obesity expert:

> I was completely uninterested in obesity. Like most people, all I had was a lot of preconceptions about it. [At the time] I was subbing on the ward in the Department of Infectious Diseases, I was basically waiting to get a residency so I could become a specialist, and then the department's funding was revoked, and I was out of a job.

Then a friend told her about a vacancy at an obesity unit at a university hospital. A phone call later, Dr. Johansson met with the chief physician at the clinic who offered her a job. "I suppose I thought 'well a job is a job.'" She laughs. "What's funny is that I had no idea what I was doing. I just didn't get it; I couldn't see why it was so difficult to lose weight. What's the problem?"

M. Forrest (✉)
Department of Social Anthropology, Stockholm University,
Stockholm, Sweden

H. Høyer Leivestad, A. Nyqvist (eds.), *Ethnographies of Conferences and Trade Fairs*, DOI 10.1007/978-3-319-53097-0_5

Nevertheless, Dr. Johansson started her new job. A month or two later she travelled to Finland to attend that year's European Congress on Obesity (ECO), a trip that came to alter her career path.

> All of a sudden I realized this is more or less a disease that people suffer from and each and every one of them is working like mad to get rid of it... It was a real eye-opener... I suddenly understood that obesity isn't caused by poor character or sloth, it's not just about informing people on what to do. The whole obesity problem is so much more complex, and genetics are powerful as well. That's when the penny dropped for me.

Dr. Johansson recounts how these realizations ultimately lead her to become passionate about obesity. When the Department of Infectious Diseases contacted her with a job offer she turned them down, choosing instead to pursue this new field. For practitioners such as Dr. Johansson the conference became a central space for awakening passion for obesity. Her attendance at this conference was fundamental to her understanding of obesity as complex medical condition, a realization, which made her pursue a career in obesity medicine. Dr. Johansson is not the only expert who described to me how fundamental obesity conferences had been in developing their interest in the condition for this very reason.

Obesity as a *complex* condition is a term constantly used when obesity experts speak about obesity and the term's relevance has also been noted by social scientists writing on obesity. Obesity as a site of expertise, as anthropologist Emilia Sanabria notes, is largely about what is not yet known, known as well as what is unknowable about the (obese) body (Sanabria 2016: 132). Conferences, as Dr. Johansson's account illustrates, are spaces in which this complexity is made evident. This chapter examines how obesity conferences act to produce obesity as a complex and multi-factorial disease and how this production of obesity in turn acts to shape obesity experts as a group who share a similar view of obesity and the obese body. Following recent material feminist writings on obesity I seek to illustrate how obesity experts unite in attempting to make sense of obesity as a particular kind of disease (Colls 2007; Warin 2015). I suggest that the conference is a site in which experts come to understand that obesity is not a simple matter of the sufferer lacking willpower but is much more complex and is even a novel type of disease which does not easily fit into the traditional medical framework. The ethnography presented depicts a

debate concerning obesity treatment that took place at obesity conferences in 2010 and 2011, through which I illustrate how the conference
becomes a site where obesity experts are mobilized and made through
their attempts to make obesity fit into a medical framework.

MAKING OBESITY A DISEASE

Conferences are by their very definition temporary, yet they hold the
potential of creating enduring change in the fields that organize them.
They are spaces where experts meet, and cement what they know as well as
what they do not yet know. Further, as Erving Goffman notes, the space of
the conference is contexts that foster academic identities (1971: 1).
Conferences are temporary spaces, which remove delegates from their
normal lives and (for this reason) may influence them differently than
they would in more familiar settings (ibid). In this way conferences can
be understood to produce expert groups.

Not only are obesity conferences spaces in which obesity specialists are
made, it was in fact through a conference that obesity became a disease.
Just one year prior to Dr. Johansson's attendance at ECO, the World
Health Organization (WHO) hosted a conference on preventing and
managing what was now to be understood as "the global epidemic" of
obesity (WHO 2000). It was at this conference that the organization
proclaimed that obesity was now to be considered a disease (ibid). In
this declaration lies a call for action, de facto summoning the medical
expert community to attempt to resolve the "obesity epidemic." Science,
as Bombak suggests, was understood to be the remedy for obesity
(Bombak 2014: 510). While the medical community has done its best to
attempt to solve the "obesity epidemic," obesity is proving to be a unique
type of disease.

Obesity as a disease carries with it a wide range of preconceptions, as
Dr. Johansson suggests to me in our interview. Such a statement is based
on a controversy regarding whether or not obesity can be understood as a
disease at all. While obesity is formally a disease there exists both within
medicine and in the social sciences some debate surrounding the diagnosis. There has been extensive criticism about the medicalization of obesity
from within the social sciences. These theorists argue that fatness has gone
from being a socially stigmatized position to becoming a disease (Gard
and Wright 2005; Monaghan et al. 2010; Rail 2012). This has to do with
the fact that obesity differs greatly from a traditional definition of disease.

The causes of the "obesity epidemic" are, according to the WHO, a consequence of large-scale environmental change (World Health Organization 2000: 1). The increase in BMI in recent decades is largely explained by a new relationship to food systems (Guthman 2011). People, in short, tend to eat more and exercise less.[1] As a consequence people develop health problems, which are caused by their interaction with the modern environment. This explanation for obesity serves to explain, at least in part, why obesity is often thought of as an individual problem of willpower, since the prevailing neoliberal idea is that we ourselves are responsible for our food intake (Becker 2013: 36; Guthman 2011; McCullough and Hardin 2013: 3).

While the explanation for the "obesity epidemic" from the WHO to some extent frames obesity as a consequence of behaviour and choice, medical obesity experts work instead to develop and understand the physiological causes of obesity in individuals. The physiological explanation of obesity, in this context, is that obesity is caused by "positive energy balance" which occurs when a person's intake of calories exceeds his/her caloric expenditure (World Health Organization 2000: 102). Thus while obesity is deemed a disease, it is a disease which is ultimately caused by the convergence of the body's normal functions with a new type of environment. Currently obesity experts are tasked to treat this new disease either by surgery or lifestyle alteration treatment as only one obesity drug (showing limited results) is currently on the market. Consequently, obesity experts today unite in spaces such as conferences to understand how the body's (normal) functions of appetite, weight regulation and metabolism can be altered either by surgical means, lifestyle change or pharmacological treatment. My ambition is neither to refute obesity experts' understanding of obesity as a disease nor to advocate this status, but rather to show how obesity experts attempt to incorporate this rather novel health state into an existing medical framework in the space of the conference.

While obesity conferences and gatherings such as workshops for obesity experts are instances that do not necessarily lead to direct change in a group they do provide "discursive spaces not normally available" within the group (Schüssler et al. 2014: 141). Obesity conferences and meetings can be seen as settings that provide a temporary interaction that does something in the group. Schüssler et al. (2014) as well as Hardy and Maguire (2010) are not the only ones to point to the relevance of temporally bounded gatherings such as conferences for a field or a group. Bruno Latour (2005) notes that meetings are an instance, in which groups are practically done, instances in which they appear. These doings are necessary for the very existence of a group. In what follows I illustrate how the conference functions as such a space.

PHARMACEUTICALS AND OBESITY EXPERTS

While the WHO conference on obesity was important in framing obesity as a disease in its own right.[2] International medical obesity conferences have been organized by non-governmental organizations since the mid-1970s[3] and have played an important part in establishing obesity as a medical expert domain. Indeed, when one of the first international conferences on obesity was held in London in 1974 it signalled that obesity was now a condition worthy of medical attention (Howard 1975: 7). This is largely because conferences on obesity act to signal that the condition is both medically relevant as well as a significant area of knowledge production. The obesity conference is a space that illustrates that obesity has become a medical issue. By their very existence obesity conferences signal that the dominant discourse on obesity today is that it is a disease (cf. Rail 2012: 228).

When obesity became a disease following the WHO conference (and subsequent publication of the strategies proposed there) a new class of people came into being through the classification. But, as Ian Hacking states, classes of people are produced "by a dialectic between classification and who is classified" (Hacking 2004: 280). Obesity conferences are sites where we may observe how classification comes about through research and debate, but perhaps more importantly obesity conferences are spaces where experts make *themselves* by agreeing on classification, treatment and the uncertainties and complexities of the same. Obesity experts unite and become a distinct group by sharing a view of obesity as a complex and multifactorial condition.

In the case of obesity, conferences can be understood as temporary installations of disease production. Invariably every obesity conference I've observed has at least one session resulting in a debate on the uniqueness of obesity as a medical condition. While medical science might be believed to be the solution to the "obesity problem," medical obesity experts are attempting to find solutions to a condition which does not fit into a traditional medical framework. Thus, while the obesity conference acts to cement obesity as a medical condition it is also a space in which the experts themselves unite in the fact of understanding obesity as medical condition different from other types of diseases. This fact is made particularly evident in conference debates and discussions surrounding the pharmacological treatment of obesity.

During a lecture at the summer school for obesity experts, Professor Stefansson, a senior expert and former president for the International Association for the Study of Obesity (IASO) expressed his dissatisfaction with the pharmacological administration's reluctance to keep drugs on the market by beginning a presentation by saying that obesity is truly a unique condition in that it alone seems to see more withdrawals of drugs than new drugs entering the market. In an interview Professor Stefansson explained: "In obesity the bar is extremely high, the safety bar. If you give people cytostatic treatment for cancer you can give them anything, as long as they survive [the cancer]. Ribonabant [an obesity drug withdrawn in 2008] was withdrawn because of six suicides and it's possible that Ribonabant saved more than six peoples' lives who would have otherwise have had heart attacks, but the bar is extremely high."

What Professor Stefansson was alluding to was the common understanding among obesity experts that because obesity was a complex condition no obesity drug worked universally on all patients; drugs generally showed low efficacy in pharmacological trails thus shifting the risk/benefit analysis. Any side effects of a drug (or any treatment for that matter) are deemed as serious if the benefits are seen to be low in relation to the risk of taking the drug. Obesity drugs have a "high bar" as Professor Stefansson calls it because they show such limited results, leaving the margin for risk very low in comparison to other diseases. This statement illustrates that obesity experts understand obesity as multifactorial. It lacks a single cause. Thus these specialists are dealing with the introduction of a medical condition that lacks a single cause and thereby does not fit the classical criteria for diseases. In *Testing Pills, Enacting Obesity: The Work of Localizing Tools in Clinical Practice*, Petra Jonvallen also notes the tendency amongst her (obesity expert) informants to categorize obesity as a multifactorial disease (2005: 159). Obesity, one of her informants noted, is caused by many different things (ibid). The fact that obesity is perceived of as not having a single cause seems to equate to the fact that obesity cannot have a single cure. For this reason, obesity appears to be a condition which does not comply with the formal testing of drugs, or at least when drugs for obesity were tested on large populations (defined as obese on BMI grounds) the drugs generally induce a weight loss of between

5 and 7 percent, a result so meagre that there is little allowance for side effects. A consequence of this is of course that drug withdrawals occur frequently in obesity, as Professor Stefansson told the experts at the conference recounted above. Discussions on the lack of medications for obesity become one of the ways in which obesity experts formulate the complexity of obesity.

Pharmaceuticals hold the promise of working as a magic bullet to alleviate suffering and repairing the body with no other process of healing involved (Petryna and Kleinman 2006: 9). This over-fetishized view of pharmaceuticals, as anthropologists Petryna and Kleinman term it, is perhaps not all too surprising, the possibility of mass producing several different agents such as penicillin, or streptomycin for the treatment of tuberculosis, mingle with other vital pharmacological breakthroughs in the twentieth century supporting the notion that medications hold the answers to the treatment of ailments no matter what these may be (Petryna and Kleinman 2006: 2).[4] But medications which cure or alleviate a disease also act to cement the belonging of a disease in the bio-medical project. The project of bio-medicine is framed by the mission of identifying firstly a cause and then a cure for any medical condition as medical sociologist Steven Epstein notes (Epstein 1998: 31). Finding treatments such as pharmaceuticals become important in establishing the disease status of any condition. Understood in this light the lack of treatment options for obesity also acts to reproduce an insecurity of whether or not obesity is a disease. This idea significantly influences what it means to be an obesity expert.

Most experts I met during my fieldwork harboured a dream of the development of a drug for treating obesity that might stay on the market. Yet the low allowance for side effects leaves obesity experts with few pharmacological treatment options, which at conferences in 2011 became tangible through negative comments toward both the pharmacological industry as a whole and the American national drug administrations, such as the FDA, in particular. Yet obesity experts are still hopeful that there will eventually be a pharmacological treatment that they would be able to offer their patients, a treatment that would offer an option to surgery, and yet be more than lifestyle intervention. In September of 2011 Dr. Johansson told me about her "obesity treatment wish-list":

> Having an alternative to surgery in the form of pharmaceuticals would be great. Something that wouldn't give too many side effects, but that seems to

be some way off. I think it's sad. Right now we're evaluating a drug against diabetes and we are waiting to see if you can lose weight on it as well, but it will probably only become available to patients with diabetes. But I'm still hopeful about a future where we can offer our patients more than just lifestyle because most patients just aren't satisfied with a couple of kilos of weight loss, they want to lose more, so that its noticeable, and that means that the changes are big, and that requires aids and crutches to lifestyle intervention...

Dr. Johansson wished for a pharmacological treatment for obesity in order to aid patients' struggles in maintaining and losing weight. A drug, she felt, would offer a crutch or an aid, which could enable larger weight loss and in so doing perhaps help patients who found lifestyle change too arduous. Yet underlying such statements is also a hope that a medication would appear (and stay on the market) which would increase the status of obesity as a medical condition. Thus the focus on the lack of pharmaceuticals for obesity treatment at conferences, and the consequent debates about obesity as complex and often misunderstood condition, must also be understood as part of the making up of obesity experts as a united group. In what follows I describe how the lack of pharmacological treatments for obesity is made tangible.

TANGIBLE ABSENCE OF PHARMACEUTICALS

Conferences become important spaces in which obesity experts unite their understanding of obesity's complexity. During 2010 and 2011 the lack of pharmacological treatment for obesity was one of the foremost issues that these experts discussed in the space of the conference. While such discussions are fuelled by the experts' understanding of obesity as a highly complex and often misunderstood condition, there is another perspective which makes the lack of pharmacological options important in the setting of the conference. A lack of efficacious treatment options lowers the status of obesity as a medical condition and, consequently, the status of being an obesity expert. Further, the lack of pharmaceuticals in obesity affects obesity conferences in more tangible ways as well: When the pharmaceutical industry lacks drugs for a condition they also remove their sponsorship from the event. This produces noticeable effects in the setting of the conference. Something that was made particularly evident when Dr. Ström, therapist Morgan, and I travelled to Orlando, Florida, to attend the Annual Scientific Meeting of the Obesity Society, the American obesity group's annual conference. Chief physician Dr. Ström, therapist Morgan, and I complained of being constantly hungry. Our lack of sustenance eventually drew us to the exhibition hall of the conference. The hall was massive, and as far as the eye could see there were stalls from commercial actors attempting to sell various aids to the medical experts attending the conference. There were stalls selling weighing scales which measured body fat, stalls that sold prototype foods which dieticians could use to illustrate caloric contents of popular food items, but also vendors selling mealtime supplements. Dr. Ström walked assertively toward the stalls selling these supplements. With a professional air she asked questions about the composition of the bars, and after a brief exchange we were handed enough samples to see ourselves through the remainder of the day's sessions.

While numerous laughs were had at the irony of experiencing hunger at an obesity conference, there was also a note of uneasiness in the observations that the conferences were so sparse in their offerings of snacks and food. Dr. Ström told me that the meagre lunches and snacks served at the conference were a far cry from the conferences of the past. This was no doubt due to a lack of funds now that pharmacological companies no longer sponsored events such as these, she speculated. Thus at the conference in Orlando the atmosphere of resentment toward the FDA for recently turning down several obesity drugs that had been in the pipeline, became particularly noticeable.

While this is an instance in which a blurring of the boundary of market and medicine becomes perceptible (pharmaceuticals although intertwined with medical practice are to do with industry and profit) (see Lakoff 2006). It also illustrates how obesity differs from other medical conditions where sponsorship from the industry is commonplace. For obesity experts this means that the conference and the social aspects that bring the group together become far less compelling. There is therefore reason to speculate that the anger against the lack of pharmaceuticals used to treat obesity is fuelled at conferences because this lack becomes so evident within them.

Thus while pharmaceuticals can be important in reformulating the very way that they understand both the body as well as a medical condition, as anthropologist Jamie Saris (2008) suggests they also hold the potential to do more than change the body of the patient. An obesity drug that actually works holds the potential of lending legitimacy to obesity as a medical domain, and similarly making obesity experts a group with resources to act.

TRIAL AND ERROR

At the eleventh International Congress on Obesity in 2010 in one of the largest auditoria at the Stockholm Fair Conference Hall, a group of high ranking members of the IASO took the stage to present the result of the trial which has led to the revocation of the drug Sibutramine, the much debated SCOUT-trial (Sibutramine Cardiovascular OUTcome trial). SCOUT was commissioned by the European pharmacological agency as a follow-up evaluation of the cardio vascular risk of the drug in high-risk patients (http://sibutramine.com/finland/sv-fi). What is novel about the trial and also one of the reasons for the uproar in the medical obesity community is that, contrary to other pharmacological trials SCOUT was only interested in high-risk patients, selecting patients over the age of fifty-five years and, in order to be deemed a high-risk patient, the participants needed to have experienced a cardiovascular event or have type 2 diabetes (James 2005: 45). The study ultimately showed that high-risk patients have an increased risk of "nonfatal myocardial infarction and non-fatal stroke" (James et al. 2010: 915). Thus the drug was taken off the market leaving Orlistat as the only drug available for obesity treatment.

Attendants at the Conference spoke of little else after the presentation of the SCOUT trial. There was uproar against the fact that yet another way of treating obesity had been revoked, due to the general lack of under-standing of obesity as a disease. Obesity is understood by these experts as multifactorial and complex. For this reason it does not fit the classical criteria for diseases. Here the conference becomes an important space for the obesity experts to formulate an impression of why the drug was with-drawn. It is in the context of the conference that obesity experts who share a similar understanding of obesity itself fuel their impression that the wider scientific community does not fully grasp the complexities of the condi-tion. Treatment options matter in the making of obesity as a complex medical condition: for experts the claim that obesity is not a single disease but several is mainly based on the understanding that treatments such as medications cannot work universally in all obese patients. Professor Stefansson, the previous president of the IASO, explained the withdrawal of Sibutramine as well as the reasons for the obesity experts' uproar about its removal in the following manner:

It's a very strange and complicated story. When Sibutramine was approved the authorities did so under the proviso that studies of the benefits of the drug in high-risk populations were to be conducted. That is how the SCOUT trial came about. So they found patients in whom the drug was really contraindicated, and the study showed that there were heart attacks in the group, none of them fatal. There wasn't any higher mortality, but a greater number of heart attacks in the treated group. And that is what the pharmaceutical company had said which is why the drug was not to be given to this group so there was this "I told you so mentality" and it didn't help that we said that we could test our patients' blood pressure and their risk factors...We thought that good doctors could handle the administration of the drug because there were many who needed it. We had patients who burst into tears when it was revoked, it took away their hunger but that didn't seem to matter.

The obesity community is in uproar about the withdrawal for several reasons: Firstly, the side effects of the drug were well established and the drug was strongly contraindicated for patients who had elevated blood pressure or heart disease. Secondly, the trial was seen as biased since it only included a high-risk group of patients who in clinical practice would never be prescribed the drug in the first place. Thirdly, Sibutramine's disappearance marked one of the central problems in obesity treatment: obesity's inability to be tested on the same grounds as other conditions, because obesity was according to experts not one disease but several, it was a multifactorial event. There is yet to be a drug that will be effective in a larger group of patients. Dr. Johansson's reaction to the withdrawal is similar:

It makes me so angry, that was the last really good drug that we had that gave very few side effects, and to test it on patient group which was far too sick and in which it was contraindicated and then to conclude "whoops, that's not so good." I think that showed bad form on the part of the pharmaceutical company and those in charge of the study in agreeing to do it. If they had to test it they should could have tested it on a group that wasn't as sick as the ones they used in the trial...I mean we can't use it on anyone with heart disease.

The example of Sibutramine provides an instance where it is possible to note the production of the scientific obese body and the disease of obesity itself (cf. Haraway 1991: 252–253). Here, a large clinical trial, a pharmaceutical company, a group of experts and any number of patients come together in order to define what counts as valid treatment and for whom. The same can be said for any available treatment option for obesity, in fact it is when the various treatment options are discussed amongst experts that ideas of obesity's complexities, boundaries, causes, and potential treatments are mapped and become tangible. The following section takes a closer look at the scientific debate of obesity treatment and how obesity experts attempt to make sense of the complexities of treating obesity.

A Site for Imagining Treatment

At the American obesity conference in Orlando I experienced an atmosphere of resentment toward the FDA for recently turning down several obesity drugs that had been in the pipeline, at a time when the obesity expert community was still smarting from the withdrawal of Sibutramine.

The conference sessions were held in the conference centre, which was part of the hotel complex where we were staying. The conference area is a built environment independent of the tropical heat and sun of Florida. The air conditioning sees to it that conference rooms are freezing cold. Devoid of windows and natural light, I was surprised at the end of the day when leaving the conference centre to discover that I was in fact in a sunny and warm Florida. Dr. Ström appeared slightly disappointed in the conference. Her impression was that this conference offered few new insights, while concluding that it is always good to attend the conference just to make sure that the treatment approaches that the Clinic offers are in line with what others in the field are doing. Statements such as this illustrate the role of conferences in obesity expertise. Conferences act as sites where experts within the field can quickly access new treatment options and make sure that the treatments they themselves offer are part of a wider scientific zeitgeist. Yet the statement also offers an envisioned feature of the obesity conference: that it will offer some new and revelatory science that changes the field in one way or another. This feature of the obesity conference is one that produces obesity experts as we have already seen in Dr. Johansson's statement about how a conference made her an obesity expert.

However, as the conference in Orlando proved, not all obesity conferences can offer revelatory insights which make and re-make expert. In these instances, conferences may act as temporary spaces that act to illustrate the state (and status) of obesity as a site of expertise more generally. Rather than offer any new insights into obesity treatment the conference in Orlando became a space in which experts summarized the current state of knowledge and treatment on obesity. This is a feature which was made particularly evident during one the conference sessions.

The session was a staged debate titled *Drugs, Surgery, or Behaviour: Place Your Bets!* The debate had the air of joviality and involved three different presenters who all represented a particular line of obesity treatment. While the debate acted to summarize the various treatment pathways for obesity that currently exist this particular session also came to offer the delegates a space in which to envision new and more effective treatments which would truly change the face of obesity as an experts' site.

The debate began with a discussion of the classical approach to obesity treatment, that of lifestyle alteration or behaviour modifying treatment, the presenter Tom O'Malley argued that obesity treatment, no matter what the treatment type, was still based on lifestyle intervention and lifestyle change. O'Malley began by outlining the problem: In order to lose weight changes in caloric intake, and lifestyle need to be made, this means eating and drinking less, a fact that is well known to us all. However, O'Malley continued, for a variety of reasons, physiological and other, this is not as easy to do as it sounds.

O'Malley went on to describe what most of the audience already knew. That obesity was a very complex condition to treat due to the changes that have occurred in food availability and food environment. O'Malley described that this new environment made obesity a highly difficult disease to treat, because human biology was in conflict with an environment which promoted weight gain. Increasingly, O'Malley argued, the term lifestyle change was taking over from the prior terms of "behaviour modification," a term which in his opinion better captured the fact that obesity was "a multi-facetted effort with multiple targets" whose treatment utilizes experts from a variety of disciplines such as dieticians, exercise specialists and behavioural specialists.

The audience listened patiently, nodding their assent from time to time as O'Malley presented what was already known to most about the so-called behavioural approach to obesity treatment. The audience was also treated to the surgical perspective on obesity treatment. During this session the presenter also offered a commonly held perspective on obesity surgery, citing the appropriate articles and statistics that illustrated the efficacies and problems that were currently held in this expert domain. In time, the microphone was handed over to yet another presenter who was going to speak about the pharmacological treatment for obesity. Dr. Carol Green of Boston University strode onto the stage with a surprising amount of energy. Surprising because it was difficult to see what she might find to say about the topic of drugs in the climate where drugs had proved so difficult to keep on the market. Yet her presentation proved very different from the other presenters in the session. Rather than speak on the success rates and features of current drugs for obesity the presentation focused on the problems of all current methods of treating obesity and suggested instead that the future of obesity treatment might well lie in the pharmacological approach.

> So I am debating Dr. Maquire on bariatric surgery? Is there a better solution than bariatric surgery? I'm debating Doctor O'Malley on behavior therapy, is it enough? So what is the argument for pharmacotherapy versus bariatric surgery or behavior therapy? So let's start with bariatric surgery. I call it an imperfect remedy. Its great! It gives you great weight loss. It costs a lot of money and there's a complication rate and even a mortality rate, even though it's low...The two biggest reasons in my mind after seeing so many patients who meet the criteria for bariatric surgery is that it's just not appealing for many of these patients but we do 250 000 of these procedures in the United States we have millions of Americans who meet the criteria for bariatric surgery and even if it was appealing to these patients it's not feasible to do surgery on all who are candidates.

Dr. Green moved swiftly on to her critique of behavioural therapy. This type of treatment shows results that are confirmed to affect the risk factors, but they are highly costly in both time and energy. The problem with the lifestyle approach to weight loss was that it was far too demanding.

> Behavior modification is very difficult to keep that up and I think the weight loss register has shown us what people need to do to lose weight and keep it off. Five thousand participants...having lost fifty pounds for at least five years and what they have to do is they have to exercise a lot, eat breakfast every day, weigh themselves once a week, and eat a low calorie diet which is very difficult to do. And the institute of medicine guidelines after reviewing the literature recommended that those who want to keep the weight off should do 90 minutes of exercise every day. That's not a big deal [laughs]...The majority of obese Americans need something in between diet and exercise and the gastric bypass...

The future of successful obesity treatment was instead to closely study the effects that gastric by-pass surgery produced in their patients, and attempt to mimic these effects in a drug for obesity. Here Dr. Green was elaborating on already well-known features of surgical treatment for obesity; the surgery appeared to alter hormones that were responsible for appetite regulation. Some of these were at the time well known, but there was a belief in the obesity expert community that there were several more hormones that the surgery influenced which were not yet fully understood. Dr. Green concluded: "We still don't know, probably don't know all the hormones involved, so it's going to take us a while to figure out exactly how to simulate gastric bypass surgery."

During the subsequent questions and answers segment of the session most questions were directed at Dr. Green. One audience member asked if she knew of any drugs at the moment that would "conquer the fattening world in which we live," a drug that didn't depend on a patient being willing to make lifestyle changes.

> Let me qualify my comments I think that there are drugs, combinations of drugs and surgery and what they do when they are successful is that they help the patient suddenly be able to make the lifestyle change that is what we are really talking about. And again most people think that we created this environment and that's why we have an obesity problem. Certainly genetics plays a big role and not all of us get fat in this environment but a significant number of us do, so right now the best option the best combination of drugs can certainly help a patient make the lifestyle changes so in the future maybe we will cure the obesity problem with a combination of drugs cause I don't think we're certainly not going to be able to change the environment.

The complexity of obesity is here formulated in terms of obesity being a condition that is both biological but also fundamentally environmental. While there were ways to treat the condition they were all according to Green both costly and time consuming. A drug that would emulate the effects of surgery (even the unknown and little understood effects of it) would thus formulate obesity as a different type of condition all together.

Two of the presenters at the session offered an overview of the current state of obesity treatment. These presentations were met by the audience with assent and comprehension, but little enthusiasm. The topics were, after all familiar, and approaches which most of the delegates worked with day to day. Dr. Carol Green, however, offered a different type of presentation. Rather than speak of the current options for treating obesity pharmacologically, she chose instead to speak about the imagined future of pharmacological obesity management. The tactic was one which harnessed the audience interest because while it presented an, as of yet unrealized pathway of, treatment it at the same time offered the experts a space in which they could use their own understanding of the complexity of obesity to imagine new and efficacious methods of treating the condition. It awaked inspiration.

Hardy and Maguire (2010) use the term "field configuring events" to denote a particular occurrence that makes a difference within a particular group at a particular time. The presentation above is an example of a field-configuring event because it aligns the already existing ideas of obesity and its complexity into a different avenue where complexity and the unknown can hold possibilities in the future. Debates among medical professionals such as these offers an instance where what is already known becomes channelled into aspirations of knowing in the future.

CONCLUDING COMPLEXITY

This chapter began by recounting how a conference on obesity made Dr. Johansson into an obesity expert. It was in the space of the conference that she came to learn that obesity was a complex medical condition. Drawing on this statement of Dr. Johansson this article has illustrated how the obesity conference becomes a site where obesity is produced as a complex medical condition. I have focused my attention on the discussion of pharmacological treatment for obesity and how obesity experts formulate themselves in response to the withdrawal of drugs for obesity.

I have argued that the lack of pharmacological treatment for obesity, the withdrawal of obesity drugs became a topic that united the obesity experts attending the 2010 ICO. The delegates were united in their view that the industry simply did not understand the complexity of obesity, which cannot be made to fit the existing frameworks of disease treatment.

Thus this chapter has suggested that obesity conferences are sites which not only serve to define obesity and its treatment but that simultaneously produce a group of experts who understand obesity as a particular type of complex disease. By following recent anthropological work on obesity I suggest that we may understand how obesity experts become a group through conferences by taking seriously how obesity experts conceive the (obese) body, the cause(s) of the condition and appropriate treatment.

Here I have suggested that in order to understand expertise and the making of groups, anthropology needs to take seriously the very objects that the experts seek to understand. The conference becomes an invaluable space for such anthropological enquiry because it unites a group that to a large extent shares a specific epistemology of obesity. The conference is a performative space where experts come together to formulate an epistemology of the obese body and how to negotiate it to fit into a medical framework. Further the temporal nature of the obesity conference means that it becomes a site where future treatments for the condition can be imagined.

NOTES

1. This is yet another example of the explanatory model of the energy-balance equation.
2. Prior to this occasion, obesity was considered a risk factor for developing disease and premature death, not itself a medical condition.
3. The World Obesity Federation (WOF) Previously the International Association of the Study of Obesity (IASO) has been an important actor in obesity expertise, partly by producing research, and by founding the International Taskforce on Obesity which worked closely with the World Health Organization to prepare the material for the meeting of 1997 where WHO declared obesity a disease. http://www.worldobesity.org/who-we-are/history/
4. The modern pharmaceutical industry, as Petryna and Kleinman (2006) note, is a venture which relies on the internationality of the different (large-scale) companies (2). Kleinman and Pertyna suggest that the nature of this global pharmaceutical industry produces a moral economy in which it is more profitable to develop drugs for the treatment of chronic (yet not life threatening) diseases in the West rather than risking non-profitable investments in areas such as anti-HIV drug markets in Africa (ibid: 2–3). Yet it would seem that when it comes to a new form of ill health which links the environment as a culprit on the bodies of humans such drugs are not easily developed or kept on the market.

REFERENCES

Becker, Anne, E. 2013. "Resocializing Body Weight, Obesity and Health Agency." In *Reconstructing Obesity: The Meaning of Measures and the Measure of Meanings*, eds. M. McCullough and J. Hardin. Oxford: Berghahn Books.

Bombak, Andrea. 2014. "The 'Obesity Epidemic': Evolving Science, Unchanging Etiology." *Sociological Compass* 8(5): 509–524.

Colls, Rachel. 2007. "Materialising Bodily Matter: Intra-action and the Embodiment of 'Fat'." *Geoforum* 38(2): 353–365.

Epstein, Steven. 1998. *Impure Science: AIDS, Activism, and the Politics of Knowledge*. Berkeley: University of California Press.

Gard, Michael, and Jan Wright. 2005. *The Obesity Epidemic: Science, Morality and Ideology*. London: Routledge.

Goffman, Erving. 1971. *The Presentation of Self in Everyday Life*. London: Penguin.

Guthman, Julie. 2011. *Weighing In: Obesity, Food Justice and the Limits of Capitalism*. Berkeley: University of California Press.

Hacking, Ian. 2004. "Between Michel Foucault and Erving Goffman: Between Discourses in the Abstract and Face-to-Face Interaction." *Economy and Society* 33(3): 277–302.

Haraway, Donna J. 1991. *Simians, Cyborgs, and Women: The Reinvention of Nature*. New York: Routledge.

Hardy, Cynthia, and Steve Maguire. 2010. "Discourse, Field-Configuring Events, and Change in Organizations and Institutional Fields: Narratives of DDT and the Stockholm Convention." *Academy of Management Journal* 53(6): 1365–1392.

Howard, Alan. 1975. "Preface." In *Recent Advances in Obesity Research: 1 Proceedings of the 1st International Congress on Obesity*, ed. A. Howard. London: Newman Publishing.

James, Philip, T. 2005. "The SCOUT Study: Risk-Benefit Profile of Sibutramine in Overweight High-Risk Cardiovascular Patients." *European Heart Journal Supplements* 7(Suppl. L): 44–48.

James, Philip W., Ian D. Casterson, Wladmir Coutino, Luc F. Nick Finer, Aldo P. Van Gaal, Maggioni, Christian Torp-Pederson, Arya M. Sharma, Gillian M. Shepherd, Richard A. Rode, and Cheryl L Renz. 2010. "Effect of Sibutramine on Cardiovascular Outcomes in Overweight and Obese Subjects." *New England Journal of Medicine* 363(10): 905–917.

Jonvallen, Petra. 2005. *Testing Pills, Enacting Obesity: The Work of Localizing Tools in a Clinical Trial*. Linköping: Linköping University Press.

Lakoff, Andrew. 2006. "High Contact: Gifts and Surveillance in Argentina." In *Global Pharmaceuticals: Ethics, Markets, Practices*, eds. A. Petryna, A. Kleinman, and A. Lakoff. Durham: Duke University Press.

Latour, Bruno. 2005. *Reassembling the Social: An Introduction to Actor-Network-Theory*. Oxford: Oxford University Press.

McCullough, Megan, and Jessica Hardin. 2013. *Reconstructing Obesity. The Meaning of Measures and the Measure of Meanings*. New York: Berghahn.

Monaghan, Lee F., Robert Hollands, and Gary Pritchard. 2010. "Obesity Epidemic Entrepreneurs: Types, Practices and Interests." *Body & Society* 16(2): 37–71.

Petryna, Adriana, and Arthur Kleinman. 2006. "The Pharmaceutical Nexus." In *Global Pharmaceuticals: Ethics, Markets, Practices*, eds. A. Petryna, A. Kleinman, and A. Lakoff. Durham, NC: Duke University Press.

Rail, Geneviéve. 2012. "The Birth of the Obesity Clinic: Confessions of the Flesh, Biopedagogies and Physical Culture." *Sociology of Sport Journal* 29(2): 227–253.

Sanabria, Emilia. 2016. "Circulating Ignorance: Complexity and Agnogenesis in the Obesity 'Epidemic'." *Cultural Anthropology* 31(1): 131–158.

Saris, Jamie A. 2008. "An Uncertain Dominion: Irish Psychiatry, Methadone, and the Treatment of Opiate Abuse." *Culture, Medicine and Psychiatry* 32(2): 259–277.

Schüssler, Elke, Charles-Clemens Rüling, and Bettina B.F. Wittneben. 2014. "On Melting Summits: The Limitations of Field-Configuring Events as Catalysts of Change." *Transnational Climate Policy* 57(1): 140–171.

Warin, Megan. 2015. "Material Feminism, Obesity Science and the Limits of Discursive Critique." *Body and Society* 21(4): 48–76.

World Health Organization. 2000. *Obesity: Preventing and Managing the Global Epidemic*. WHO Obesity Technical Report Series 894. Geneva, Switzerland: World Health Organization, 1.

CHAPTER 6

The Biennial of Dakar: Scales of Art Worlds-Networks

Thomas Fillitz

INTRODUCTION: THE BIENNALE OF DAKAR AS FIELD-CONFIGURING EVENT

In 1989, Senegal's President Abdou Diouf founded the Biennale of Dakar. Within a two years cycle, it should alternate between a biennial for authors/poets (first edition 1990), and a biennial for visual arts (first edition in 1992). This presidential decision followed a long-lasting lobbying of Senegalese artists, who were searching the challenge with international peers. Due to the high commitment of the visual artists, only the biennial for visual arts was to survive. Whereas it was launched in 1992 according to their intention as the *Biennale Internationale des Arts*, the Senegalese state appropriated it from the outset as a platform for its cultural politics in an international perspective. In as far as this Biennale edition was not successful, and considering the insight of state

Acknowledgment I am particularly grateful to the *Biennale de l'art africain contemporain*, Dak'Art, for supporting my field researches in 2008, 2010, 2012, 2014, and 2016.

T. Fillitz (✉)
Department of Social and Cultural Anthropology, University of Vienna, Vienna, Austria, WU

© The Author(s) 2017
H. Høyer Leivestad, A. Nyqvist (eds.), *Ethnographies of Conferences and Trade Fairs*, DOI 10.1007/978-3-319-53097-0_6

107

officials and major art world professionals not to replicate some international biennial models, such as the one of the Biennale di Venezia, the Biennale was re-directed to becoming the *Biennale de l'art africain contemporain* (Biennale of African Contemporary art), with its first edition in 1996. This decision, however, was not accorded with the artists who had lobbied for the mega-event, and the latter were not pleased with this decision.

The foundation of Dak'Art, the Biennale of Dakar, corresponds to a period of proliferation of art biennials all around the world, a movement that intensified by the early 2000s. Nowadays, one may speak of a world culture of art biennials – the notion of biennial referring to a specific type of temporary art event, whether its temporary cycles are biennial, triennial, or longer. Anyone can be founded upon decision of a state, a city, or of private institutions, and it focuses on contemporary art that either relies on the determination of the European/North American art world, or it is regionally specifically defined. Biennials form a world culture in as far as they constitute a global circuit, cyclical clusters, as Power and Jansson have detected for trade fairs (Power and Jansson 2008: 423). Besides features which are generally mentioned–travelling artists and art works, internationally acting curators, and an international travelling art public–they are informally connected in as far as the art biennial format is the major characteristic of the present-day art worlds-network (Vogel 2013).

This chapter investigates the Biennale of Dakar, Dak'Art, as a "Field-Configuring Event" (Lampel and Meyer 2008). (1) The biennial is a nodal cultural space bringing together artists, curators, art specialists, and an art public with highly different geographical backgrounds. (2) It spans over one month every two years, from early May to early June. (3) Especially during the first week of each edition, it provides opportunities for intense face-to-face interactions between various art world actors. (4) Besides the exhibition spaces and the forums of debate, activities include the ceremonial grand opening, multiple exhibition openings, and receptions. (5) Dak'Art has constituted itself as the platform for visualizing and debating the newest trends of contemporary African art. And (6) via its selection procedures and other mechanisms, the Biennale contributes to the validation and valuation of contemporary artistic practices that are on display. With its particular focus on "contemporary African art," that is selected artists in the international exhibition -need to have a citizenship of an African state, Dak'Art reveals itself as a showcase for those artists who "recognize and accept their African origin" (Konaté 2010: 117).

Before proceeding, I need to discriminate between art fairs and art biennials (see also Tang 2011). Art fairs are inherently connected to the art market, most of them being economically oriented corporations. They are events in which selected galleries exhibit artists they have under contract. Their duration is several days, and their cyclical cluster follows a clear yearly calendar, thus enabling potential buyers to attend all major ones. Art fairs centrally focus on profit making. The most prominent art fairs have major bank corporations as partners, have sponsors for most activities, and galleries pay huge fees for renting stalls. There is a clear global hierarchy between art fairs for contemporary art, the most prominent being Art Basel (with Art Basel Miami and Art Basel Hong Kong), and Frieze Art (with Frieze Art London and Frieze Art New York). Art fairs clearly focus on potential buyers, in particular on so-called "High Net Worth Individuals," for whom special visiting times and glamorous events are organized. This clientele is attracted on the grounds of galleries with international reputation, which ensure a high-end diversified supply of artworks. The art-interested public is welcome on the basis of relatively high ticket prizes (see Fillitz 2014).

Art biennials belong to art worlds. Their focus is on the creation of artworks from different regions, and are thereby fundamentally different from art market interests – by and large, they are not spaces for selling artworks. Generally speaking, galleries should have no influence on which works of art will be on display. The foundation of a biennial is closely connected to cultural reflections, often connected to cultural politics. Although dealt with under an umbrella notion, there are different models for art biennials (see among others Bydler 2004; Gardner and Green 2013; Niemojewski 2010). Curators, artistic directors, or selection committees are responsible for the quality of contemporary art in the official exhibition spaces. While sponsoring is welcome, art biennials are not as profit oriented as art fairs. Regarding their temporality, art biennials last for a longer time, a month for the Dakar Biennale, 100 days for documenta in Kassel, or from June to mid-November for the Biennale di Venezia. Their cyclical calendar is not that clearly structured as the one of art fairs, often biennials may overlap in time. Their focus is on various actors–artists, curators, gallerists, art specialists, critics, collectors and the art-interested public. From a European/North American perspective the Biennale di Venezia and documenta are on top of the biennials' hierarchy. I, rather, suggest a more differentiated view, considering for instance the Bienal de la Habana as being most important for the global South,

Istanbul for the connection between Europe and the Middle East, or Dakar for Africa. Also, biennials, in particular those of the various South(s), are most relevant for local or regional art worlds in many respects–be these art practices, art criticism, local art markets, or the formation of an art-interested public.

Considering formats of biennial, a closer examination of the Biennale of Dakar shows that it specifically fulfils several tasks: since the time of first President Léopold Sédar Senghor, culture has been a central factor for the Senegalese state's ideology. It relies on connecting democracy and modern culture for promoting the image of the country at the international level (Nzewi 2013: 26). The Biennale thereafter constitutes one of the illustrious events for promoting Senegal's international cultural politics. This, nevertheless, does not imply that Dak'Art is "a search for nationalist publicity and tourism," as Tang is suggesting for art biennials (Tang 2011: 79). There are other important viewpoints to be considered in this context, insofar as the Biennale is emphasizing clearly art related aspects. From the Biennale's viewpoint, it is first the showcase for contemporary African art; it is, second, a platform for scholarly debates and exchanges; third, the Biennale contributes to the professionalization of artistic practices, of art criticism, the development of collectors and art sponsorship, of the art market; and fourth, it focuses on art education in schools and universities (Fall 2009, 2010; Fillitz 2012).

This chapter discusses several scalar networks Dak'Art produces to these ends. I argue that Dak'Art constitutes a cultural institution[1] that consciously stretches out to the world culture of biennials, to African art worlds, and within Dakar's art world. In the first part I consider the productions of symbolic capital. With its institutionalization as *Biennale de l'art africain contemporain* (Biennale of Contemporary African Art) in 1996, Dak'Art had to be recognized at a global level for the valuation and validation of works of art created by African artists. To these ends, the nominations of each selection committee were central. Another aspect of its symbolic capital showed to be related to sites. Not any place for exhibition was considered as equally apt for the display of contemporary artworks. Third, from its beginnings several institutions are awarding prizes to artists for their works. All artists I talked to consider them as most important for enabling further research of their practice, for achieving a better international visibility, for their network building.

The second part examines the Biennale as a space of encounter and its strategies for network building. I shall focus on three of them. First,

Dak'Art has been following an invitation policy that is furthering the gatherings of artists, art specialists and the art-interested audience. Second, the Biennale not only focuses on exhibitions, much effort is allocated to the organization of different spaces of debates that also should contribute to professionalization of art related occupations. And finally, Dak'Art emphasizes art education of youths, and brings schools into its central show, the international exhibition.

THE PRODUCTION OF SYMBOLIC CAPITAL

The Selection Committees

From 1996 on, Dak'Art relies on selection committees for the international exhibition. The Secretary General nominates its members after discussions with the committee of orientation.[2] Until 2006, these committees were quite large, around ten members per edition, and there was a balance between members with an African citizenship, or an European and a North American one (Fall 2002). All of them are art specialists, being among others (museum or exhibition) curators, critics, gallerists and artists. Generally, the Secretary General and the President of the committee of orientation too were members of it.

From 1996 until 2006, the presidents of these committees were prominent international curators, such as the Italian Achille Bonito Oliva (in 1998), or the British David Elliott (in 2000). As first Secretary General Rémi Sagna (acted between 1996 and 2000) explained to me, this was a conscious strategy for raising an awareness of this newly created biennial within the world culture of biennials, while at the same time aiming at assuring the quality of the presented artworks. In 2006, the Biennale decided to nominate for the first time an African general curator, the Ivoirian Yacouba Konaté, who was free to invite his curatorial team. Only from 2010 on, members of the selection committee had to have a citizenship of an African state—wherever they lived—and in 2016, the internationally most renowned curator Simon Njami was appointed as artistic director with the exclusive responsibility for selection. While many other biennials rely on the system of general curators, these selection committees fulfil several tasks of the Biennale as Field-Configuring Event—aspect (1), the selection of artists, aspect (5), the display of the newest artistic practices, and aspect (6), the validation and valuation of artistic practices.

While this former strategy of inviting non-African art specialists into this committee raised indignation among local artists and art specialists, in as far as they lacked in majority any knowledge of modern and contemporary African art (see also Fall 2002), one needs to acknowledge this decision as a strategy of the Biennale to constitute connections into the global art worlds-network, and to position itself as a global cultural institution beyond its exclusive focus on contemporary African art. During the Biennale's 10th edition in 2012, I discussed with Simon Njami about this relationship between global visibility and curators. His opinion was straightforward: an internationally renowned curator for sure attracts the interest within the global art worlds-network: "It is, however, mandatory to know whom to approach for such a task." The shift towards an exclusive African curatorship should not be considered as a strengthening of regionalism. By 2010, the Biennale was successful in being globally acknowledged as the biennial for contemporary African art. The impact of African art specialists needed to be intensified, in particular their in-depth knowledge of African art worlds.

The Importance of the Site

It is Saturday, May 10, 2014, and together with a friend I pick up a taxi to rush towards the opening of the international exhibition. For this 11th edition of Dak'Art, a space in an industrial zone of the city has been selected. Following the instructions we received, we arrive at the place–but where is the Biennale? No advert, no logo of the Biennale! Other people arrive and look around as we do. A youth approaches us, and asks whether he could help us. Yes, "we are searching for the Biennale of Dakar!" He interrogates some of his fellows, and then indicates to us: "It's behind this white wall, you need to enter through the gate over there!" We meet some acquaintances from former editions, and our first concern was: truly, this was hard to find.

This year's Dak'Art had rented the premises of a media corporation. For most of the former editions, Dak'Art was hosted within the premises of the Musée Théodore Monod, also known as Musée de l'IFAN in the center of Dakar. As one of the curators later told me: "We were searching for a larger exhibition space that would allow for more flexibility, a space that would not be museum like." Many local artists I talked to however did not appreciate this decision: "This is not a place worthy of hosting art, this is an industrial zone, it has nothing to do with art," as one of them angrily exclaimed.

Dak'Art's main venues, what is called Dak'Art IN, actually consists of several exhibition spaces, the international exhibition being the core of the Biennale. This is the exhibition where the artworks of the officially selected artists are on display, and art critics prominently focus on it for the evaluation of the Biennale. In 2016, artistic director Simon Njami was successful in appropriating for this exhibition the ancient *Palais de Justice*, inaugurated in 1958. For Njami, this building constitutes a real contemporary space, and connects to Senegal's art history in as far as it hosted the contemporary art show during Senghor's *1er Festival Mondial de l'Art Nègre* (1st World Festival of Negro Arts) in 1966. It further is emblematic for the 2016 Biennale's theme, "The City in the Blue Daylight," which is a line of a poem of Senghor. Whether artists, art critics, or the art public I talked to, all were delighted of this location. As artist Pascal Nampémanla Traoré expressed: "Fantastic! We needed to get out of this museum [Théodore Monod, note of the author], and this exhibition shows the potential of this location for the arts."

These discussions about the site of the international exhibition refer to its importance in relation to the valuation and validation of contemporary art, particularly aspect (6) of the Biennale as Field-Configuring Event. Formerly, art museums acted against the uncertainty connected to contemporary art creation, and contributed to the validation and valuation of a work of art, whether it was incorporated in one of its shows, or, better, if it enters into its collections. I realized at Dak'Art that these mechanisms are also closely linked to the reputation of the exhibition space. This becomes more obvious in considering the other space of the Biennale, the so-called Dak'Art OFF. This is an open, free space for exhibiting, without any central selection or any exclusion mechanisms, and where selling too is a major interest of artists. Exhibitions of the OFF rely on initiatives of individual artists, of international cultural institutes–such as the *Centre Culturel Français*, the Goethe Institute, or British Council–, of galleries, small art institutions, or of corporations. Suffice to find a location, and that may also be offices or private homes, hotels or restaurants, petrol stations, and so on. The Biennale's secretariat only takes care in collecting the information about exhibitions, and of producing a guide of them.[3] In 2016, there were around 300 such exhibitions.

Although Dak'Art OFF is conceived as fundamentally popular and egalitarian, there are nevertheless particular sites with a high symbolic value for artists. The *Galerie Le Manège* of the *Centre Culturel Français*, the galleries Atiss, Kemboury or Arte, the corporation Eiffage Sénégal, or Raw Material Company and *Atelier Céramiques Almadies*, for instance, are famous locations for exhibiting artists with reputation. Openings of these events are a "must," and the highest numbers of visitors, and most major players of the local art world come together during these openings.

The sites of the Dak'Art IN produce on the one hand the symbolic capital of contemporary art in Dakar. On the other, it specifically contributes to a better international visibility of the selected artists. Prominent exhibitions of Dak'Art OFF too enhance the symbolic capital of exhibited artists. Senegalese artist Cheïkhou Ba, for instance, started an international career after having been included in a remarkable collective exhibition in the OFF in 2004, and his peer and friend Barkinado Bocoum was invited to the second edition of the biennial of Casablanca (October 2014), after its curator had seen his OFF-exhibition during the 11th edition of Dak'Art in 2014.

The Prizes

The awarding of prizes is a major component of art biennials, and they are not only the recognition of an extraordinary artistic practice, they too influence an artist's status on art markets. The first biennial to abolish prizes was the *Bienal de la Habana*. The curatorial team of the Wilfredo Lam centre considered prizes as a competition among peers, which would create an atmosphere that went against the emphasis of "getting together and exchanging ideas" (Llianes 2000: 13).

Dak'Art is awarding prizes from its beginning. At the end of the grand opening ceremony, representatives of the prize-awarding institution honour the selected artists. In doing so, the Biennale fulfils several aspects of a Field-Configuring Event, namely the ritual of ceremonies (4), and the focus on validating and valuating specifically the awarding artists (6). One needs, however, to discriminate between the various prizes that are awarded at each edition. The most important one is the Grand Prix Léopold Sédar Senghor, later also called *Grand Prix du Chef de l'État*. Generally, the President of the state is giving the prize. The second in importance is the prize of the Ministry of Culture, also called *prix révélation* (prize of revelation), handed over by the Minister of Culture, then follow the prize of the *Organisation Internationale de la*

Francophonie, the prize of the city of Dakar, and other prizes awarded by art foundations, such as those of the French *Fondation Blachère*.

On the basis of the exhibited artworks in the international exhibition, a special jury (sometimes the selection committee) is deciding the prizes connected to the state, the city of Dakar, or the international organization of the Francophonie. Art foundations have their own selection decisions. Prizes, moreover, consist in a diploma and either an amount of money, or they take the form of residencies in a European art centre.

The hierarchy among prizes corresponds to different intentions. The Grand Prix Léopold Sédar Senghor is awarded to artists who have achieved some fame, and it is a recognition of their work. The revelation prize of the Ministry of Culture rather is awarded to a younger, most promising artist, while the prizes of art foundations are mostly helping artists to intensify and elaborate their artistic practices, whether they have already some standing or whether their achievements are promising.

Officials of Dak'Art do not consider prizes as a tool for producing hierarchies, or for creating a strange atmosphere, as the curators of Habana conceived them. Quite on the contrary, they see them as most important for contributing to the status of artists, for their promotion in local, regional, or international art markets, and, in the case of residencies, for an intensified exchange with artists in Europe. As former Secretary General Ousseynou Wade stated: "Prizes are most important to us! They contribute to the international career of an artist, they encourage and promote practices of younger artists. Residencies, for instance, are really extremely helpful in this regard." For Senegalese artist Barkinado Bocoum the *prix révélation* of the Ministry of Culture in 2010 had major consequences for his career:

> It was intended as residency in France. I, however, asked them to give me the money so I could work, and they did so. It further contributed to a better international visibility. I got invitations for residencies in France and Belgium, and I was invited to exhibitions in Europe. It really helped me a lot to advance in my career!

I too observed many times how artists were pleased with their honoured colleagues. There is a strong collective impetus at Dak'Art, and many artists consider these prizes also as an overall valuation of contemporary African art. In this context, the production of symbolic value may be related to Moeran's and Pedersen's concept, highlighting here specifically its social, situational, and appreciative dimension (Moeran and Pedersen 2011: 12).

SPACES OF ENCOUNTER AND NETWORK BUILDING

The Biennale of Dakar fulfils two encompassing purposes, positioning itself within the world culture of biennials, and at the same it highlights itself as a particular space of encounter within the local art world. It thus aims at establishing its uniqueness through strategies of stretching out to the global level, attracting an international attention among art world members, while constituting spaces of encounter for artists and art specialists from Africa and its Diaspora. With these plural foci, Dak'Art aims at being the biennial of contemporary African art, as well as the central cultural institution for the local art world. Besides the role of the committee of selection, the Biennale has been focusing throughout its history on the production of its public.

The Production of the Public

Basically all venues of Dak'Art are free for anyone. Although the Biennale insists that VIPs, gallerists, collectors, artists, art specialists, and art world members need to be accredited for accessing all events, the badge is mostly required for the grand opening ceremony, yet for none of the other ones. In all the years I attended Dak'Art, there was only one visitor's survey of Dak'Art IN in 2008. Accreditation therefore may also be considered as a means of the Biennale to get information about the international art world public. For 2012, Dak'Art's website informs about the participation of representatives of the Biennale di Venezia, Dubaï Art Fair, La Biennale de Lyon, the festival Videobrasil de São Paolo, of, among others, Centre Pompidou, Tate Gallery, Newark Museum, the National Gallery of Nigeria, or the Royal Ontario Museum, of various art centres and galleries. In 2016, a prominent local art collector and curator informed me about the visit of the director of the Museum of Modern Art/New York with six of his collaborators (Dak'Art 2016).

Besides "official participants"–sponsors, art professionals and art amateurs, media, and the selected artists–, the survey of 2008, presented by Youma Fall in a talk in Germany (2009), reveals as public 140 international artists and 312 Senegalese artists, all having exhibited in the OFF, 230 collectors and art "amateurs" (Africa and Europe), 690 international art professionals (Africa, Europe, America and Asia), 520 tourists (Europe and America), 1400 from schools and universities in and around Dakar, while the local public was identified as "insignificant" (Fall 2009: 4). A first interpretation of these data reveals four major aspects, the interest of international professional art worlds' members, the participation of members of the local art world, a focus on schools and universities in Grand Dakar, and the missing of a local public.

Together with a group of students from my department I conducted a small survey as a means for orientation. The survey was done during four days at the international exhibition at Musée Théodore Monod (starting with the second day after the opening[4]), and during two hours in the morning with a questionnaire we had developed. A total of 105 questionnaires were analyzed, nonetheless interviewees did not answer all questions. Visitors we interviewed were living in Senegal, Martinique/Guadeloupe, Canaries, France, USA, Switzerland, Germany, Belgium, Canada, Italy, Spain and The Netherlands.

This small orientation survey shows: in the overall perspective, regarding age, visitors are in majority rather young. All of them have accomplished an education, most of them from universities. The interest in Dak'Art is firstly contemporary art, then specifically contemporary African art, and a bit lesser degree the OFF. This coincides with the time spent for visits, mostly between one and four days, however many as well mentioned up to ten days. Senegalese interviewees differ from the general perspective in as far as all have occupations directly connected to art, fewer express their interest in the OFF, a third of them mentioned as reason of visit their residence in the city, and a third would spend more than 22 days for visiting the Biennale's premises.

Three overall aspects seem determinant in this production of the public. One needs to consider, first, the local public, second the Biennale's concentration on Dakar, and third, the impact of the international art audience. I often heard artists arguing to stretching out the Biennale beyond Grand Dakar and covering the whole Senegalese territory with art activities, in order to better bring in the local population. As late Amadou Sow told me a few years ago: "Dakar is successful regarding its international attendance, now we need to go a step further, we need to go to the people and to include other sites within Senegal!" It is also an often heard critique from state officials that the Biennale does not serve its citizens, and only connects to the global art worlds-network.

But what is meant by "local public"? The survey presented by Youma Fall (2009), and our small one both clearly show the interest of artists, as well as of local art world members who are living in Grand Dakar. "Local public" thereafter may be defined as Senegalese citizens who have yet not developed an interest in contemporary African art. In Youma Fall's explanation: " ... the visual arts in their contemporary version are a kind of graft that has yet not been picked up in the African context"[5] (author's translation).

This phenomenon seems, nevertheless, to be an average one. Simon Sheikh calls this failure of reaching out to the local audience the "lack of local sedimentation" (Sheikh 2010: 157), and it concerns most of the contemporary biennials: "Indeed, one of the most widespread complaints about contemporary biennials is their lack of connection to the 'local audience'" (ibid: 157). Regarding documenta in Kassel, a survey of documenta 11 (2002)[6] shows quite similar patterns as the data presented from Dak'Art: only 7 percent of Kassel's population visited the event, younger people were the majority (20–39 years), a third of the visitors were academics, and only a little more than 1 percent skilled workers (Ketteritzsch 2007).

The state's argument is obvious, in as far as it addresses this "local public" in terms of citizenry. Again and again state officials provocatively wonder why such a high budget should be spent for an event that is mainly of interest for an international public, but that by and large is not attracting the Senegalese population. For art professionals, and art-interested people, the question rather relates to the development of the local art world. In claiming that the Biennale should appropriate various sites in Senegal, they focus on a larger, truly national Senegalese art world. Contrary to Tang's consideration of biennials as institutions serving to intensify tourism (Tang 2011: 79), these perspectives clearly underline that for this particular Field-Configuring Event, tourism *per se* is neither in the focus of the Senegalese state, nor of local art world professionals.

Discussing the topic of the "local public", and leaving apart the added value of this event for Senegal's tourism economy, one needs to also include within such reflections the impact of Dak'Art OFF. By now Dak'Art is the combination of the IN and the OFF. The latter has expanded to various locations in and around Dakar, and since the early 2000s, the OFF in St. Louis du Sénégal has developed to being the second centre of the Biennale. Joëlle le Bussy, President of the *Association pour la Promotion des Arts Visuels d'Afrique* and director of Galerie Arte (Dakar and St. Louis), coordinates the events in this location. St. Louis offered 41 exhibitions in 2016, while the OFF in Dakar and its neighbourhoods presented around 300. Former Secretary General Ousseynou Wade (from 2000 to 2012) acknowledges the importance of the OFF for the overall perception of the Biennale: "One has to rethink the IN in relationship to the ever growing OFF. In which way is the IN still the flagship of the Biennale?" Mauro Petroni, who coordinates the production of the OFF-guide from its beginnings in 2002, argues that this space is popular in as far as the majority of its exhibitions are in non-art locations, and whoever wishes may present her/his art creations. I actually attended many openings in the OFF, where I observed that people who just passed by got curious, and had a glance at the show.

Dak'Art's production of the public thereafter may be differentiated into three major fields. The IN is the space that connects to the local art world, and an international public pre-eminently from Africa, Europe and North America. This is the field on which the Biennale's office focuses centrally. The second field is the one of the most prestigious sites of the OFF, those worthy of contributing to the symbolic capital of the exhibiting artists. Here too one finds this same public. It is an art-educated audience with interests in contemporary art in general, and specifically in contemporary African art. The third field consists of the many not so prestigious, and non-art locations of the OFF. This is the popular side of the Biennale. Its public is more heterogeneous, and consists of members of the local art world, possibly some of the international visitors, more so friends and acquaintances of those exhibiting, business partners of those providing the premises, of customers of these locations, and a few people who simply pass by.

Network Building

Dak'Art's production of the public is closely connected to several strategies that the Biennale applies, and which contribute to connecting with the world culture of biennials, to network building with other regional and local African art worlds, to the local art world for the professionalization of its various members and for a future rise of interest in contemporary art within the local population. These are the Biennale's invitation policy, the platform of debate *Rencontres et échanges* (encounters and exchanges), and its focus in bringing in schools. Gardner and Green consider such "gatherings of artists, commissioners, writers and publics from within and outside a given region" (Gardner and Green 2013: 450) to be a characteristic of Southern biennials. It too is a characteristic of the Biennale as Field-Configuring Event (aspect 3). Since 1996 the Biennale has been following a policy of inviting official participants, artists and international art world professionals, taking in charge their travel, accommodation, and local transportation during the first week. According to Konaté, this amounts to 30 percent of the Biennale's overall budget (Konaté 2009: 79). For the editions of 2014 and 2016, Royal Air Maroc became the official partner for assuring the travel of the selected artists and art world professionals–such as curators, art theorists, art journal editors, gallerists–, who participate in the platforms of debate. In doing so, artists are present at the international exhibition, they stand next to their works, and are eager to discuss with anybody approaching them. The Biennale moreover lodges them in the same hotel in order to create the best conditions for interaction. "This is a fantastic experience! We stay together in the same hotel, we look at each other's work, we visit together exhibitions, we discuss our respective practices . . . " an artist told me. It is a special atmosphere that establishes the Biennale as a real space of encounter. Artist Barkinado Bocoum, explained:

> When I was selected in 2010, the Biennale told us local artists that we should stay in our homes, that there were enough possibilities to interact with our peers. I said no, I wanted to stay in the hotel with the other artists. This would enable me an in-depth interaction, and the Biennale agreed. This is was what we are looking for!

Several local artists mentioned that these interactions were specifically important for getting acquainted with new media, for being able to discuss questions of artistic practices with colleagues who come with their respective experiences. "I left Dakar in 2002 because I was interested in new technologies for my art. Now these are quite usual here. Dak'Art is fundamental for these exchanges with African artists who live in other regions of the world, for developments of our own art practices," states artist Cheikh Niass who is working by now with multiple media.

For several editions by now, many other international art worlds' specialists join in at their own expenses, so do artists who exhibit in the OFF. They too enjoy and value the Biennale for the possibilities of network building, be it with other artists, gallerists, curators, art theorists and critics. During the 2016 edition for instance, Rosalie van Deursen, an independent curator of the OFF exhibition "Urban Africans–*Les artistes briseurs de tabous*"[7] at the Dutch Embassy, organized talks between art students and the local artist Kine Aw, to use the exhibition for intensified reflections about artistic endeavours.

The Biennale actually not only focuses on the exhibition spaces with its invitation policy, much attention is paid to organizing platforms of debate, such as *Rencontres et échanges*. Spanning over a period of several days during the first week, it allows to discuss with the curators about their selection, about present trends of contemporary art, about other biennials or art festivals, about art sponsorship, about the self-marketing of artists, about art publishing. This field is mainly for art specialists, although open to anybody, and Dak'Art considers it a duty for contributing to the professionalization of the local art world – the focus being, among others, its artists, gallerists, art foundations, collectors, art theorists and art critics (see also Fall 2010: 182). One actually needs to consider these multiple tasks and strategies of the Biennale in the context of difficult circulations of artworks, artists and art world professionals in Africa, or the aspirations for communication and exchange among these art world actors.[8]

In Youma Fall's survey the high number of schools is of special interest. In all editions I attended, I was astonished of the large number of school children of all ages who could be seen in the premises of the Biennale's exhibition from the end of the first week on. At several occasions I observed teachers discussing with school children what artists are, what they are doing, what a curator is. I observed how they were talking in front of specific works of art, how they were encouraging them to express what they were seeing, how they drove their attention to particular characteristics of an artwork. I too observed elder school youth with pencils and writing pads, walking around in the international exhibition, and taking notes here and there. One day in early May 2014 I discussed these observations with the third Secretary General, Babacar Mbaye Diop, who was responsible for the 11th edition in 2014.

> This is most important to us! We need to develop art education in schools, in order to raise the interest in contemporary art of the youth. It is our initiative. The Biennale makes appointments with the schools, and we are using our budget for hiring the busses to bring them here.

In several public debates, as well as in personal discussions with local art world members, this initiative was often addressed as the need for learning "to read a contemporary artwork." This strategy of the Biennale clearly focuses on the upcoming, young generations to develop a sensibility for contemporary art, and it affects local school curricula. It also connects to visitors' surveys that reveal that in majority younger people appreciate the biennial format.

CONCLUSION: MULTIPLE FACETS OF DAK'ART AS FIELD-CONFIGURING EVENT

Many artists, who had been lobbying for a biennial of visual arts in Dakar since the mid-1980s, were unhappy with the government's decision in 1993 to create a biennial of contemporary African art, they instead wanted a truly international one. This decision nevertheless enabled the Biennale to clearly position itself within the world culture of biennials. On these grounds, Dak'Art had to build itself as a centre for a specific South-South circulation of African artists and their artworks, and thereby raising a particular consciousness among them. From its beginnings the Biennale moreover had to contribute to the development of the local art world, as well as of Dakar's art market.

These various tasks the Biennale has to fulfil, were primarily considered within the framework of the Field-Configuring Event. I thereafter applied the latter's criteria as established by Lampel and Meyer (2008) to the Biennale. Although the Biennale's periodicity is longer than the one of trade or art fairs, and that the Biennale is not primarily market sales oriented, Dak'Art's strategies nevertheless show similar characteristics as Field-Configuring Event. Its brings together artists, art world professionals and art amateurs, particularly with its invitation policy, it cultivates its festival character with ceremonies like the Grand Opening, its central intention is to confronting visitors with newest trends of contemporary African art, and, specifically with its awarding of prizes, it emphasizes the valuation and validation of selected artistic practices.

I examined in this chapter on the one hand the production of symbolic capital regarding contemporary African art at large, and more specifically for the artists' careers. On the other, I considered the construction of spaces of encounter, of the gatherings of art worlds' members for network building.

The production of symbolic capital, understood as recognition of Dak'Art within the world culture of biennials, is first connected to the nomination policies of the selection committees. Calling in prominent European and North American specialists served two interrelated intentions. It was meant to contribute to a better global visibility, and it was a means of basing the validation and valuation of contemporary African art achievements within an international framework. The shift towards an exclusive African curatorship from 2010 on may be seen as a reaction to critiques of African artists and specialists. By the time, Dak'Art moreover had been acknowledged as being the showcase *par excellence* for contemporary African art. This new practice then corresponds to an enhanced self-confidence. The Biennale was successful in its regional focus while connecting to the world culture of biennials. It moreover was a step further in acknowledging African art specialists' roles for curating, and for actively shaping the valuation of African art practices.

For nearly all of its editions, the main venue of Dak'Art IN, the international exhibition, was hosted within the complex of the Musée Théodore Monod in the centre of the city. This was not by coincidence. Local artists and art world professionals actually are according the site of displaying contemporary art a major symbolic importance. This became most apparent, when the selection committee of the 2014 edition chose as main venue of Dak'Art the site of a broadcasting company in the industrial zone of Dakar. Although this space allowed for more flexibility, could host more artworks, and would not contribute to a "museification" of contemporary art, this choice was heavily critiqued as being a non-space for visual arts. When international renowned curator Simon Njami succeeded in presenting the international exhibition of 2016 in the former *Palais de Justice*, all art world actors I talked to were amazed. The connection between the valuation of contemporary art and the site where it is shown, the symbolic capital thus produced, is also visible in the prestigious institutions within the OFF-space.

The Biennale further actively contributes to the production of symbolic capital of artists with its strategy of awarding prizes. Though there is a hierarchy between them, these prizes however are not considered as producing competition between artists, thus hindering their interaction and exchange of experiences. Quite on the contrary, artists view their positive contribution for intensifying artistic research, for getting an international visibility and contacts with art institutions in other art worlds.

Regarding interconnections, the Biennale applies several strategies. The most important one is the Biennale's invitation policy. In doing so, Dak'Art is constructing itself as a space of encounter. This ensures an atmosphere of intense interactions and discussions between artists, art specialists, and an art-interested public. Its foci relate to different dimensions of knowledge, be these art practices, art theory and critic, and expands to various aspects of the local art market. The other stronghold of the production of the public is the Biennale's activity for raising the sensibility for contemporary art. By bringing in schools, teaching youth "to read works of art," Dak'Art's officials set a clear sign for the future of the local art world.

In this context, a contested topic is the inclusion of the local public. Local people who visit the exhibitions of the IN, or join in on its platforms of debate, are members of the local art world. As the presented statistics revealed, this audience is an educated and rather young one, and has occupations that are closely connected to art. The "lack of local sedimentation" (Sheikh 2010 [2009]: 157), actually is not characteristic for this particular biennial, it is a widespread phenomenon. One needs to acknowledge for one that an art world for contemporary art is a specialized field within a society, and nowhere is comparable to popular or mass culture. This becomes obvious with the attribution of symbolic capital to the sites of the Biennale–be it for the IN or the OFF. In considerations of artists and other local art world members this corresponds to a demarcation from other societal fields. The "local public" thereafter should be restricted to members of Dakar's art world. It is not a matter of an overall citizenry, as the state's critique suggests. The question rather is about developing this art world, as artists view it, but the Biennale alone cannot solve this issue.

With each edition, Dak'Art consciously produces several scalar networks. These so established various interconnections define its uniqueness, that is, its character as an African nodal cultural space, as well as its specific position within the world culture of biennials. Around the common interest in contemporary African art, the Biennale as space of encounter thus attracts participants centrally from Dakar's art world and from Africa and its diaspora, with specialists and art-interested actors from other regions of the world. Its particularity finally is constructed with the complementarity of spaces of exhibition–the curated ones of the IN, those of the prestigious sites of the OFF, and the self-organized ones of the OFF–with platforms of debate, and possibilities for intense interactions among various art world actors with different geographical background.

NOTES

1. A notion I borrow from Born (2010).
2. The Minister of Culture appoints the members of the committee of orientation by decree. This committee is responsible for Dak'Art's overall agenda, such as budget and sponsorship.

3. Since 2004 Eiffage Sénégal has been sponsoring the *Guide des exposants* (guide of exhibitors).
4. During this time, most art world professionals are present, whereas schools start visiting the Biennale from the end of the first week on.
5. "...les arts visuels dans leur version contemporaine sont une sorte de greffe qui n'a pas encore pris dans le context africain" (Youma Fall 2009: 4).
6. The administration economist Gerd-Michael Hellstern, University of Kassel, and his team investigated this survey.
7. "Urban Africans – The Taboo Breaking Artists," a small show with artworks of Kine Aw (Senegal), John Kamicha (Kenya) and Ephrem Solomon (Ethiopia).
8. The examination of Dak'Art's various tasks within the local art world thus leads to different conclusions than Tang's more general consideration of biennials, according to which the author proposes "to contest the rhetoric that these events should be a primary inspiration and investigator of sustainable networks, education, commissions, infrastructure and exchange" (Tang 2011: 87).

REFERENCES

Born, Georgina. 2010. "The Social and the Aesthetic: For a Post-Bourdieuian Theory of Cultural Production." *Cultural Sociology* 4(2): 171–208.

Bydler, Charlotte. 2004. *The Global Art World Inc. On the Globalization of Contemporary Art*. Stockholm: Acta Universitatis Upsaliensis and Figura Nova Series 32.

Dak'Art. 2016. "Dak'Art, la Biennale incontournable." Press Release. http://dakart.net/dakart-en-chiffres/ (accessed February 26, 2016).

Fall, N'Goné. 2002. "Compromise and Conflict, the Shift of African Art. Compromise and Conflict on the International Art Scene: The Shift of African Art From Margins to the Centre." *Resartis*. http://www.resartis.org/en/meetings__projects/meetings/general_meetings/2002_-_helsinki/n-gone_fall_-_compromise_and_conflict_the_shift_of_african_art/(accessed September 9, 2015).

Fall, Youma. 2009. "La Biennale de Dakar: Impact social et culturel." Conference held at the University of Erfurth (Germany). https://www.yumpu.com/fr/document/view/36075809/dr-youma-fall-confacrence-et-discussion-a-universitac-erfurt- (accessed September 9, 2015).

Fall, Youma. 2010. "Dak'Art: Transplant or Adaptational Model?." *Dak'Art 2010. 9ème Biennale de l'Art Africain Contemporain*. Exhib. cat. Dakar: 182–186.

Fillitz, Thomas. 2012. "The Mega-Event and the World Culture of Biennials: Dak'Art, the Biennale of Dakar." *The Event as a Privileged Medium in the Contemporary Art World, Maska 147–148*: 114–121. ["Megadogodek in Globalna Kultura Bienalov; Dak'Art, Dakarski Bienale." In *Dogodek kot Priviegirani Meddij na Podrocju Sodobne Likovne Umetnosti. Maska* 147–148: 106–113].

Fillitz, Thomas. 2014. "The Booming Global Market of Contemporary Art." *Focaal* 69: 84–96.

Gardner, Anthony, and Charles Green. 2013. "Biennials of the South on the Edges of the Global." *Third Text* 27(4): 442–455.

Ketterizsch, Peter. 2007. "Kunstfans kommen wieder." *Hessische/Niedersächsische Allgemeine*. Kassel, May 18. https://de.wikipedia.org/wiki/Documenta (accessed April 9, 2016).

Konaté, Yacouba. 2009. *La Biennale de Dakar. Pour une esthétique de la création africaine contemporaine—tête à tête avec Adorno*. Paris: L'Harmattan, La Bibliothèque d'Africultures.

Konaté, Yacouba. 2010 [2009]. "The Invention of the Dakar Biennial." In *The Biennial Reader*, eds. Elena Filipovic, Marieke Van Hal, and Solveig Øvstebø. Bergen: Bergen Kunsthall and Ostfildern: Hatje Kantz.

Lampel, Joseph, and Alan D. Meyer. 2008. "Guest Editors' Introduction. Field-Configuring Events as Structuring Mechanisms: How Conferences, Ceremonies, and Trade Shows Constitute New Technologies, Industries, and Markets." *Journal of Management Studies* 45(6): 1025–1035.

Llianes, Llilian. 2000. "The Havana Biennial." In *Das Lied von der Erde*, ed. René Block. Kassel: Museum Fridericianum.

Moeran, Brian, and Jesper Strandgaard Pedersen. 2011. "Introduction." In *Negotiating Values in the Creative Industries. Fairs, Festivals and Competitive Events* ed. Brian Moeran and Jesper Strandgaard Pedersen. Cambridge: Cambridge University Press.

Niemojewski, Rafal. 2010. "Venice or Havana: A Polemic on the Genesis of the Contemporary Biennial." In *The Biennial Reader*, eds. Elena Filipovic, Marieke Van Hal, and Solveig Øvstebø. Bergen: Bergen Kunsthall and Ostfildern: Hatje Kantz.

Nzewi, Ugochukwu-Smooth. 2013. *The Dak'Art Biennial for the Making of Contemporary African Art: 1992–Present*. Druid Hills/Atlanta: Emory University and PhD Dissertation.

Power, Dominic, and Johan Jansson. 2008. "Cyclical Clusters in Global Circuits: Overlapping Spaces in Furniture Trade Fairs." *Economic Geography* 84(4): 423–449.

Sheikh, Simon. 2010 [2009]. "Marks of Distinction, Vectors of Possibility: Questions for the Biennial." In *The Biennial Reader*, eds. Elena Filipovic,

Marieke Van Hal, and Øvstebø. Solveig. Bergen: Bergen Kunsthall and Ostfildern: Hatje Kantz.

Tang, Jeannine. 2011. "Biennalization and Its Discontent." In *Negotiating Values in the Creative Industries. Fairs, Festivals and Competitive Events*, eds. Brian Moeran and Jesper Strandgaard Pedersen. Cambridge: Cambridge University Press.

Vogel, Sabine B. (ed.). 2013. "Globalkunst – Eine neue Weltordnung." *Globalkunst – Eine neue Weltordnung, Kunstforum* 220: 12–59.

CHAPTER 7

Beyond Informality: Intimacy and Commerce at the Caravanning Trade Fair

Hege Høyer Leivestad

INTRODUCTION: COMMERCE AND INTIMACY

Linda and Johan's caravan is parked in a steep slope, propped up with pieces of wood underneath to ensure the right levelling. In a humid drizzle of early autumn weather, Johan–a man in his mid-30s from western Sweden–and his father-in-law are carrying wooden sticks and cans of spray paint to apply on the damp grass to make sure all arriving caravans are parked on strict, neat lines. As the two of them explain, they will not have anyone come and claim that their provisional caravan site is not in proper order. It is September 2011, and for the second year in a row, the family is appointed hosts of their local caravan dealer's temporary camp "village" outside the Elmia Trade Fair in the Swedish town of Jönköping. Linda's mother, who back home in a small town close to the Norwegian border often hangs around the caravan dealer with her friends and helps out at sales events, has now sold tickets to 60 families and assumed the responsibility of serving food and provide a party with live music and dance on the temporary campsite area. Together with her husband she started camping in the 1970s, and during the last year's fair they bought their tenth caravan model.

H. Høyer Leivestad (✉)
Department of Social Anthropology, Stockholm University,
Stockholm, Sweden

© The Author(s) 2017
H. Høyer Leivestad, A. Nyqvist (eds.), *Ethnographies of Conferences and Trade Fairs*, DOI 10.1007/978-3-319-53097-0_7

Their retailer's so-called "village" camp is one of many on the enormous grass fields surrounding the large trade fair buildings, and it is where the local Caravan Club section hosts 8,000 camping guests during the second week of September. For some hectic days, around 35,000 people will have passed through the interior halls of the trade fair, where new caravan and motorhome models are launched, and manufacturers, retailers, organizations, journalists and caravan enthusiasts meet to sell, seal and socialize under the headline of the mobile living industry.

Linda's family's rather curious retailer camp on the ground outside the trade fair building invites us to explore how commerce and leisure can interrelate in new–and perhaps unexpected–ways. In this chapter I take a closer look at how economic and social practices take shape at the caravanning trade fair. By ethnographically approaching a specific Swedish trade fair, *Elmia Husvagn och Husbil* (Elmia Caravan and Motorhome), I look at how the fair becomes a sphere where the selling of dwellings take place through a continuous reproduction of "like-mindedness" in an environment characterized by close connections between retailers, manufacturers and customers.[1]

As management scholars and others have shown, trade fairs gather and organize people and material objects within structures of temporary economies (Aspers and Darr 2011; Lampel and Meyer 2008; Moeran and Pedersen 2011). In the case presented in this chapter, the trade fair–as a temporary organized sphere of leisure and commerce–forms part of and produce what I will call an *intimate economy* (Wilson 2004). With intimate economy I refer to "the integration of social and economic systems" (Wilson 2004: 8), through the way aspects of intimate daily life, in this case particularly those of family relations, friendship and leisure, form part of wider economic processes. As Wilson shows in her study of commerce in Thailand's capital Bangkok, the intimate is "features of people's daily life that have come to seem noneconomic" (Wilson 2004: 11) referring to "the deeply felt orientations and entrenched practices that make up what people consider to be their personal or private lives and individual selves" (2004: 11). Already here a contradiction seems to appear. How can the trade fair, as a large-scale gathering in an apparently anonymous fair hall, be a location where this intimacy comes to the fore as a central component of commercial practice and industrial identity?

In this chapter, I will first discuss the caravan industry and the methodological approaches made possible in the trade fair setting. I also show how – at the caravanning trade fair – class is introduced with reference to a "traditional" customer. The second half of this chapter suggests that layers of intimacy are built into the ways in which relations are established and commerce is run at the fair. I thus use a specific commercial location–the caravanning trade fair-while moving between and beyond pre-given categories such as "customers," "retailers" and "manufacturers"- in order to analyze the interactions between economic and social life (Wilson 2004). As Gudeman argues in a recent book: "Economies are strange because they juxtapose self-interest and mutuality" (2016: 1). In the building of relationships between customers, caravan brands and those who manufacture and sell, the boundaries of these pre-given categories are increasingly blurred, and this leads us beyond a pure informal-formal dichotomy when trying to understand the workings of market exchange. In the next section however, I will start off by explaining the role of the trade fair in the caravanning industry.

THE LEISURE VEHICLE INDUSTRY AND THE TRADE FAIR

The European caravanning industry, boasting an annual turnover of more than 12 billion Euro, consists of actors that are involved in production and sales of touring caravans, motorhomes, mobile homes, as well as suppliers of specialist parts (such as air-condition systems). This motorized camping sector, which grew rapidly in post-war Western Europe in the 1950s to 1970s, has in the past decades experienced periods of economic difficulties related to oil crisis, increasing popularity of charter holidays, and more recently an economic recession leading to diminishing sales in large parts of Europe (Leivestad 2015). In 2015 and 2016 however, the caravanning industry boasted increasing sales, and in late summer 2015 the European Caravan Federation reported that the European Leisure vehicle sales were "skyrocketing" with a total sales rise of 10 percent.

A few years earlier, in 2010 and 2011, when I did fieldwork at the Elmia caravanning trade fair in Sweden, one had however only started to register a careful optimism among industry actors after years of heavy recession. At the 2010 trade fair press conference, the leisure vehicle trade organization's president could also proudly announce the brand new statistics from the European Caravan Federation that Sweden for the first time had overtaken Holland as the country with most caravans per capita: 291 per 100,000 inhabitants. The large amount of active caravanners in addition to a rather steady economy positions Sweden as a central market for the European caravanning sector. However, compared to some of its

European counterparts, Sweden still holds a minor position as leisure vehicle manufacturer. With four manufacturers, all of which started as family businesses and located in regions far from the big cities, some of them were at the time of my fieldwork also struggling economically.[2] The annual Swedish trade fairs are important locations for the Swedish industry, here in a sphere of competition with other European manufacturers that operate through retailers on the Nordic Market.

The Elmia Caravan and Motorhome trade fair has been arranged on the outskirts of the mid-size Swedish town of Jönköping since the early 80s. The location of the fair thus resonates with that of many others, because as Moeran and Pedersen (2011) shows, trade fairs have moved inside the exhibition halls on the outskirts of town and have thereby also become less visible to the general public. The Caravan and Motorhome trade fair in Jönköping however continues to attract visitors, not only from the local area, but from many parts of Sweden. In 2015, the trade fair hosted 35,000 visitors and 156 manufacturers in exhibition halls measuring 33,000 square meters. In economic terms the trade fair holds great importance, since as much as 20 percent of the industry's total sales take place during the trade fair. As the largest caravanning trade fair in the Nordic region, the gathering attracts manufacturers and suppliers from large parts of Europe, organizations and journalists, in addition to hundreds of Swedish retailers and thousands of potential customers and enthusiasts.

The Elmia trade fair forms part of a much larger network of European leisure vehicle trade fairs that subsequent one another throughout the year in relation to the main caravanning summer season (see also Skov 2006). The largest, *Caravan Salon*, is held in Düsseldorf in late August, early September–and with 12 halls of more than 210,000 square meters and 560 exhibitors, the German trade fair is the mega event where the latest trends and new inventions for the following year's summer season is put on display. Just a week after the Düsseldorf trade fair the Elmia trade fair is arranged in September, launching the forthcoming year's new models and allowing for orders in time for the holiday season (Leivestad 2015; Skov 2006). Thus these trade fairs are also expressions of how commercial seasons coincide with natural seasons, in an annual cycle of consumption and organization of leisure (Daniels 2009; Leivestad 2015; Shove et al. 2009). In the next section I will briefly discuss how the trade fair can be approached methodologically through ethnographic fieldwork.

Strolling the Trade Fair: A Brief Note on Methodology

While gathering actors from different parts of industries and thus offering a unique opportunity for ethnographic research of market encounters, a trade fair also provides the anthropologists with a range of methodological challenges. One is the actual possibility of prolonged contact with people in a strictly temporally bounded environment (Moeran and Pedersen 2011; Skov 2006), another is the constant movement that characterizes a trade fair. During my fieldwork at the Elmia trade fair in 2011 and 2012, at regional trade fairs (2010–2016) and the Düsseldorf trade fair (2011) I attempted to use the encounters between the materiality of the caravan and the people engaging with it as a point of departure for manoeuvring the trade fair. This implied however, shifting positionalities on behalf of the fieldworker throughout the days of attendance, ranging from press conference attendance, conversations and interviews with manufacturers and retailers, party and hang out with caravanners and tagging along with journalists.

Most important for my trade fair fieldwork has however been the employment of *strolling* the fair as a methodological strategy. Similar to modes of so-called "walking ethnography" (Cheng 2014; Ingold and Vergunst 2008) *strolling* is a method that through walking and moving along with one's informants engages with the intersections of mobility and materiality (Elliot et al. 2017; Leivestad 2017). At the caravanning trade fairs I introduced myself to caravanners by the trade fair entrance and asked if I could join them as they strolled the trade fair looking at new caravan models. On other occasions I encountered caravanners, such as Linda and her family that we met in the introduction to this chapter, at the trade fair camp or in the queue waiting to enter, and was later invited to join them during the subsequent days at the fair. While strolling the fair halls means moving along, often in slow-paced walking, in the tempo and direction of one's informants, it also implies critical stopovers. These trade fair stops are the stands of the different brands and retailers, where one enters the caravan or motorhome to inspect its qualities, while simultaneously engaging in conversations with other visitors or retailers. The next section discusses the relationship between class and caravanning through the ways caravan customers are imagined and approached at the Elmia trade fair.

In a Realm of "Like-Mindedness"

"Welcome to the New Year's Eve for camping people." The headline, displayed next to a photo of persons of different ages dressed in a variety of leisure gear–an elderly couple with backpacks, a child in swimming gear, a clown, a motorcyclist, a cyclist, a climber and a young family with children–features the website of the 2016 edition of *Elmia Husvagn och Husbil*. By visually presenting what at first glance seems to be a variety of people of different ages, backgrounds and interest profiles, the trade fair visitors are imagined as active Swedes, all joined for a weekend through their common interest in leisure vehicles.

The Elmia trade fair's advertisement strategy reflects a more general class ambivalence wherein the Swedish caravan and motorhome industry is located. As caravanning gained popularity as a leisure form in large parts of Western Europe in the 1960s to the 1980s, in countries such as the UK and Sweden its position in the public imaginary became intimately connected with stigmatized working-class culture and practice. Some decades later, these rather negative or ridiculed associations with working-class leisure continues to be regarded as a challenge for actors within the caravanning industry, leading to strategic attempts to broaden the image of the "typical caravanner." However, while manufacturers of leisure vehicles, and owners of campsites, see the need of attracting other–and perhaps economically stronger–customer groups, the image of the classic caravanner as "traditional," backwards and less open to change, is actively reproduced within the industry itself, not least at the trade fairs.

In 2010, during the press conference for the 29th edition of the Elmia trade fair, the increasing interest among manufacturers and public was perceived of as a positive trend after two difficult years of economic recession. The caravan trade association president, a suit-wearing male in his 60s, was particularly enthusiastic: "the mobile living becomes more and more interesting (...) motorhomes attract a new group, those who are slightly older. Born in the 40's like myself. The house is ready, the kids are out. And one has realized that the boat is too much work." The trade association's president refers to what he calls "the new camping people" as less sensitive regarding the state of the market. "These new motorhome owners are different," he claims. "They move! The caravanners on the other hand are a stable group," he continues, "But it takes them longer to 'change up' (*byta upp sig*), they buy a new car before they renew their caravan." In this talk, the trade fair association's president tries to establish a contrast between old and new camping people, by differing between the new and economically strong motorhome enthusiasts, and the traditional caravanners.

Still, at the trade fair, other industry actors more explicitly argue that the camping people are a rather homogenous group. During the 2011 edition of Elmia, dressed in a red waistcoat with the name of her magazine on the back, the chief editor of the most read caravan magazine in Sweden reveals to me that they call their readers "Bosse and Mona." She continues "Bosse and Mona are 55+, maybe even 60+, they have a steady economy, the kids have moved out. We know all about them from which payment card they use to whom they vote for. And these are the ones that are here. Couples holding hands, with a high average age." In a power point presentation intended for internal use that she later sends me, "Bosse and Mona" made as the typical profile reader of their magazine, are presented as being married for 25 years, living in a single-family detached house in a smaller Swedish village, with working-class or lower-middle class occupations, a rather steady economy and with an interest in motor vehicles. The image of the typical caravanner that frequent the caravanning trade fair also circulate in different shapes in other parts of the caravanning industry. At a dinner during an event for the European campsite organiza-tion, a Swedish industry actor revealed to me that he "detested" places like Elmia and the people there. "Where are the dreams of travelling?" he added. While the caravanner is portrayed as "traditional," there are indus-try actors that also reflect on the homogeneity among the manufacturers and retailers. In the late hours of the Friday night at the Elmia trade fair in 2011 I am accompanying the representatives and caravan salesmen to the hotel bar where they all gather during the nights of the fair. Seated next to me are the head manager and one of the owners of two of the largest caravan manufacturers in Sweden. One of them, a Norwegian business-man that came into the caravan business a few years before, whispers this over the table: "I mean, where are the immigrants? You can't see a single one of them. There aren't any at all in this business. This is the last bastion." The company owner's observation referred to the white dom-inance of the European caravanning industry. He furthermore reflected around the fact that the Swedish industry largely is built on family firms and has not been open to change in the ways of running business.

For some industry actors that are present at the trade fair, the connec-tions between the leisure vehicles they are trying to market and sell and a stereotyped image of a "traditional" working-class caravanner is however deemed as problematic. A sensitivity towards this image is also visible in the Elmia trade fair marketing material that in front of the 2016 trade fair stated on their webpage: "Here you can meet like-minded people with experiences from destinations, products and other things. This is a place where people that are passionate about the same things meet." But while the trade fair is announced as a location for "like-minded" people, the trade fair organizers also use the webpage with the intent to broaden their customer group. On an info page intended for manufacturers and retailers it says: " It is no longer only the traditional caravanner that visits the fair, but a variety of other groups, the family with children, the active adventurist and the active senior." The image of the traditional caravanner that circulates among actors at the trade fairs is thus both ambiguous and complicated. As I will show in the following section, by focusing on the negotiations over caravan interior that take place at the trade fair, it is however also an image actively used and taken into account when leisure vehicles are both manufactured and marketed.

INTERIOR NEGOTIATION

When I first join Linda and Johan at the Elmia trade fair in 2010 we start off with a tiresome stroll in the trade fair halls. Linda and Johan, who have a daughter of six and usually spend time in their caravan for a month in the summer and during weekends, bought their current caravan at last year's fair and had it delivered in April this year. The caravan had cost them 390,000 Swedish Crowns,[3] a considerable amount of money, and was funded with a mortgage. They had been able to order some extra comforts to their caravan when buying it at last year's fair, for instance an extra stove with oven, which does not come as standard equipment. They have also added an 83 watts solar panel to be able to manage without electricity. "You get comfortable," Johan smiles, "you can get all kinds of facilities in these caravans now." While entering and looking at new caravan and motorhome models, Linda and Johan are mostly eager to get to the Cabby stand. Their mission is a double one. While curious to see the new models of their favourite brand and talk to the retailers and manufacturers, some of whom they already know quite well, Linda has also a more serious matter to take care of. During this last summer they have discovered a bulge in the floor of their brand new caravan that they bought and ordered on the last year's fair. At the Cabby stand Linda hugs the salesmen from her local retailers, talks loudly and shares jokes. Linda also works in sales, currently in ice cream and Aloe Vera, a business that isn't going too well. Her husband Johan mostly keeps in the background, carefully attentive to his daughter, and his mobile phone. As foreman at a real estate company, he can't take too many days off. While Johan has only been a caravanner for a few years now, it is Linda who knows most of the people at Cabby, including the owner of the local retailer where Linda's family has been customers for years.

For Linda there was never really any other option than a Cabby caravan, since it always had been the favourite brand of her parents. Her father, Linda explains, literally "hates" *Kabe*, Sweden's largest caravan manufacturer and Cabby's fiercest competitor. But the bulge in the floor in her brand new Cabby caravan has made her angry. Linda is thus determined to get hold of Jonas, the sales manager from the Cabby factory, who sold her the caravan last year, and she literally bursts into the glass-walled room where Jonas is meeting a customer. Finally, somewhat sweaty, Jonas takes Linda into one of the exhibited caravans in order for her to explain the damage, which turns out to be a manufacturing problem that Cabby was already aware of. He promises that her caravan will be fixed, and Linda, now slightly more content, tries to persuade him to buy ice cream off her. A proper Cabby ice cream would be brilliant, she argues. While Jonas promises to think about it, we are moving on to look at new caravan models.

Linda and her family's connection to a particular caravan brand is not unique. Swedish caravanners actively take part in a wider discourse around the connection between material quality and particular brands that becomes activated at the trade fair, which is a space where these different brands–and their aficionados–are made visible to each other within the bounded sphere of the halls and its exteriors. In addition to reflecting brand identity, differences between good and bad caravans are often put in national terms, where ideas about material quality and design become attached to specific ideas about "Swedishness" (Leivestad 2015). While Cabby aficionados such as Linda will dislike the Swedish competitor Kabe, she would still hold that in terms of material quality the Swedish caravan is in general superior to the cheaper German models. This way of linking material quality to specific national products is one that is actively produced by Swedish manufacturers and retailers. I will return to the point of connections between customers and specific brands in the next section when discussing how relationships between caravanners, manufacturers, retailers and caravans are re-enforced through notions of intimacy at the temporary campsite.

Inside the trade fair halls however, Linda and her family continue to circulate among the caravans to observe new technological solutions, interior designs and layouts. Inside a Cabby caravan model similar to their own they quickly look around, open cupboards in the kitchen part and sit down in the sofa. Linda also moves towards the back to have a look at the layout of the beds. The beds are often a critical point for caravanners when looking at new models–and for manufacturers when constructing them–because most prefer not having to climb across their partner to get in and out of bed. Conversations around the interior layout of the caravan thus address issues of intimate family life and how to manage relationships in a domestic sphere of limited size. The material inspections of caravans furthermore take form in gendered ways, as the women I met on trade fairs tended to concentrate on the interior layout of cupboards and kitchen solutions, as well as dinettes and bedroom layout, while the men worry about the space of exterior compartments and the technical solutions of heating and electricity. Such inspections of caravans, while addressing the issues of sleeping, socializing, cooking and living, take place in a semi-public sphere of the exhibition, where customers and retailers move in and out of caravans. The more popular models can easily be crowded and the immediate intimacy of bodies cramped in the mobile dwelling trigger conversations and comparisons around solutions and camping life. Such conversations not only include the potential customers, but also manufacturers and retailers that circulate between the different caravan models in order to inform and sell.

While inside the Cabby similar to their own, Linda and Johan are introduced to a retailer from another part of the country than themselves. While first exchanging a few phrases around their wish of turning in to a newer or bigger model and the new designs, the salesman draws on his own story. He has been a caravanner since 1970, and bought a Cabby when he and his wife had a daughter. "But now I'm on my own," he sighs, "at home I mean, I don't know if it was the Cabby she didn't like or what it was." The salesman tells Johan and Linda that he travels a lot, never stays over in hotels, only in the caravan, he sleeps much better there. The community part of it is so important, he adds. And now when the trade fair has closed for the day he can just walk down to the campsite and someone will invite him to sit down. Linda agrees that the community is important and invites him to join them at the party on Friday night. Linda laughs and tells him about the vodka bottle they shared when arriving the campsite the other day.

When methodically strolling the halls with different caravanners at a number of caravan and motorhome trade fairs I observed similar processes of interior negotiations, taking place in encounters coloured by notions of familiarity. Manufacturers and retailers would often, as in the example from the Cabby stand, draw on their own family life and connection to the caravan brand when engaging in conversations with potential caravan customers. In the case with Linda and Johan, we see how the retailer engages in a conversation that–when relating to his own relationships and family history–rapidly transgresses conventional boundaries of economic exchange. The notions of intimacy that are evoked in this and similar caravan encounters feed into a larger discourse of the caravan industry as "community" that is reproduced by caravanners, retailers, manufacturers and other industry actors present at the trade fair. Through inspections of caravans that take shape as encounters inside the caravan space and include conversations over family life and relationships, intimacy becomes part of the way in which economic possibilities and transactions are understood and performed (Wilson 2004). In the next section I will discuss how the ties and attachments between potential customers and particular brands are enforced at the temporary campsite outside the trade fair halls.

Village Encounters

In its official program, posted online, the Elmia trade fair is presented as consisting of two parts: one being the exhibition of caravans, motor-homes, mobile homes, camping gear and specialized supplies, the other being "the social festival" where people enjoy themselves during four days' time. In the online posted program, the project manager of Elmia Caravan and Motorhome trade fair argues that "the trade fair is the caravanners' counterpart to Dreamhack or the Roskilde festival."[4] When tickets for the temporary campsite were launched online in February–more than six months in advance–the 1500 pitches at the most popular area closest to the trade fair halls sold out in only four minutes. The day before the actual trade fair takes place, there is a triple filed queue of cars waiting to enter the temporary campsite area. Already allowed inside the gates are only 90 caravan club volunteers, as well as some of the retailers and manufacturers that also stay at the campsite area during the days of the fair. Some of the experienced Caravan Club[5] members are however not too impressed by the crowds of people waiting outside the gates. Last year, the whole parking lot outside was full several days in advance and one lady actually queued from Saturday morning, four days before the gates of the campsite opened. But when assuming they are queuing to get the best plots I am wrong. "Oh, no we are actually placing the ones that get in first on the plots furthest away," a man in his 50s that is in charge of the volunteers laughs, claiming that this is known to all of the caravanners as well. The volunteer explains that many of the caravanners belong to clubs and are placed in what they call *byar* (villages), and all large caravan and motorhome brands and clubs have their own village. The official opening of the campsite gate and the drive-in has rather become quite a thing, he says, "a kind of tradition."

Linda and her family are also queuing outside the gates, even though they all have their pitch booked at the retailer's village they are managing, at the very far end of the green open fields that constitute the temporary campsite. In the introduction to this chapter I described how Linda's family was occupied with arranging the spatial layout of the campsite, in order to provide linearity to the parked caravans. The caravans are positioned in rows, and at the far end of the retailer's camp a party tent has been put up to provide a space for socializing during night-time. One of the side entrances to the massive grey trade fair building is only some minutes away, and as most other visitors, Linda and her family spend the days strolling the fair halls, then return to their caravan in the afternoon to have a beer and socialize.

In 2010, on the Friday afternoon of the Elmia Caravan and Motorhome, I am joining Linda and her family at their retailers' camp to help out at the night's party. As I arrive, music streams from the large loudspeakers placed outside the party tent and some of the volunteers are about to move chairs and tables to the communal space of the temporary camp. Tonight's performer is a singer that also stays over in a caravan in the retailer village. Placed in a camping chair outside Linda's caravan with a beer in my hand I am introduced to a Norwegian couple in their early 60s, friends of Linda's parents. The man has been a long haul driver all over Scandinavia and loves camping life, he tells me. Linda's mother and her friend are carrying out the food that is to be served in front of the caravan. The retailer village hosts 60 caravans, 120 adults and 50 children, and nearly all have bought a Cabby caravan from the local retailer in Western Sweden. As the evening advances and the trade fair closes for the day, the salesmen arrive, accompanied by some of the manufacturers from the Cabby factory and a competing retailer. Some of them have already had a beer or two and the conversation amongst them revolves around who actually sells the most. During the Elmia Trade fair all retailers that sell the same brand compete internally, and the central organization of Cabby awards prizes to the best salesman per day and per week. Dance band music entertains the crowd, and the owner of the retailers has entered the stage in a duet with the female singer. "It's not the dance band we are particularly fond of," he later tells me, "It's the nice songs. Where you can hug and just be fond of each other." As the manufacturers and retailer employees dance and talk with the caravanners, there is a steady and high intake of alcohol. "But," Jonas, the sales manager from the Cabby factory tells me, "even if people drink a lot, Elmia is still the most important weekend during the whole year."

As the early autumn night sets in, it starts to rain and I'm invited into Linda and Johan's caravan, where a far from sober Jonas is about to do an examination of the bulge on their caravan floor. Jonas steps on the floor, gets down on his knees to inspect more closely with his hands, and concludes that the problem might have been worse than he initially anticipated. Some form of economic compensation is mentioned before we move on into Linda's parent's caravans. Cramped into the sofa salon part of the caravan, in-between seven male salesmen and one female, we are served whisky and wine. Linda's mother has tears in her eyes, impressed that she can host the management of Cabby caravan in her own home on wheels.

This last example from the retailer village camp at the trade fair camp-site shows how a wide range of actors are gathered in forms of socializing that extend the commerce of the trade fair into its exterior space. The organization of the trade fair camps, where caravanners sleep, eat and socialize in villages that are connected to specific brands, could be read as an elaborate marketing strategy, in terms of facilitating contact and sustaining relations with potential or long-standing customers. We see however, that the building of brand identity in this context relies on reciprocal relations between caravanners, manufacturers and retailers. Here, trust and loyalty to a specific brand, such as that shown by Linda's family, relies on a continuous familiar dialogue with industry actors. These dialogues, as illustrated also in the previous section, involve the mutual and intimate sharing of camping experiences and personal family life. The ways that relationships are built and sustained–inside the trade fair halls and at the trade fair camp–thus blur the pre-given categories and divisions between producers, distributors and consumers. When the sales manager Johan performs a late-night inspection of Linda's caravan during the party, it shows how economic exchange and negotiation not only contain notions of informality, but how caravan exchange in this context is built on the very notion of intimate encounters. Hence, the trade fair becomes a space where an industrial identity of familiarity and intimate economy is both produced and made visible (see Chapter 1 in this volume).

TRADE FAIR INTIMACY

In a recent book on economy and anthropology Stephen Gudeman draws on an example from his own car purchases to provoke what he calls "the puzzle of the presence of sociability and ritual in material life" (2016: 6). In this example the salesperson always comes in at the moment of hesitation on part of the potential customer, reassuring and attentive, with compliments or even invitations to a weekend in Las Vegas (Gudeman 2016: 8). "The ritual of sociability supports yet opposes the market transaction, while the contractual connection is seemingly independent of the rapport but requires it," Gudeman argues (2016: 9). In this and other texts, what Gudeman does so well, is to point to what he identifies as the tensions of economy, where economy is always a "shifting combination of competitive and mutual relationships" (Gudeman 2016: 4).

As Gudeman also notes, it has taken anthropologists some time to take their understandings of non-western and small-scale economic contexts to also to make bearings in making sense of so-called developed market economies. In this chapter I have engaged with a specific trade fair, a Swedish caravan and motorhome fair, in order to show how industry identity can be produced and economic exchange performed in a temporally and spatially bounded sphere located at an interface of leisure and commerce. Trade fairs are central parts of how the leisure vehicle industry and caravanning sector is organized on a European level. The Swedish trade fair thus forms part of a wider network of fairs that are all regulated in an annual cycle that resonates with summer being the high–season for caravan use (see also Skov 2006). While the Elmia Caravan and Motorhome trade fair holds importance in economic terms for Sweden's caravan manufacturers and retailers, it is also one of the central locations for the launching of new models, sharing of technology and knowledge, as well as the sustaining of relationships between different actors in the industry. This is an industry, I have argued, that in large parts relies upon an image of their customers as "traditional," when referring to them as backwards or reluctant to change. However, in this Swedish context, the caravanning sector also reproduces itself through maintaining particularly close relationships between manufacturers and retailers of specific brands–and their customers.

Research on similar large-scale gatherings has shown that "elements of festivity" since medieval times have been part of the trade fair phenomenon (Aspers and Darr 2011: 760). At the caravanning trade fair this "festivity" (Aspers and Darr 2011) and "spectacle" (Moeran and Pedersen 2011) has become part of the official program, as the trade fair not only arranges stage entertainment and children activities, but also a trade fair campsite that is marketed as a "social festival." In this chapter I have shown that the trade fair thus extends into its outdoor exterior, where not only visitors to the trade fairs, but also industry actors drink, eat, party and socialize as temporary neighbours.

That "off-stage" or "backstage" networking–for instance over food and drinks- is an essential part of the way knowledge is gained and business is dealt with at large-scale professional gatherings has already been demonstrated in a range of different settings (Aspers and Darr 2011; Lampel and Meyer 2008; Moeran and Pedersen 2011). Anette Nyqvist shows particularly well in her chapter in this volume how networking actually becomes a formal part of the program at the conferences where she did fieldwork. The trade fair and the caravanning industry presents us not only with an entirely different ethnographic setting than those found in the examples above, it also forces us, I argue, to question an analytical slippage into a separation between formal and informal economy (see Hart 1973, 2005, 2006). Looking at how caravan market exchange is performed in the trade fair setting, an opposition between the formal and the informal is challenged. The ethnography presented in this paper rather points to a specific altering of private and public that builds on the ongoing connection-making between industry actors and existing or potential customers. The negotiations that take place inside the trade fair halls when caravans are inspected and evaluated, as well as the encounters among music and drinks at the temporary campsite, form part of what I have chosen to term an intimate economy (Wilson 2004). The trade fair not only makes visible the very workings of this intimate economy, but is a location where it actually emerges as a central feature of this particular industry.

NOTES

1. This chapter departs from my doctoral research on European caravan dwelling (Leivestad 2015), which was based on fieldwork on campsites and within the European caravanning industry. I did fieldwork at the Elmia trade fair in Sweden 2010 and 2011, the regional caravanning trade fair in Stockholm annually from 2011 to 2016, Caravan Salon in Düsseldorf in 2011, and the caravanning fair at the Mets in London 2012.
2. In 2015 Cabby Caravan – after years of strained liquidity- were forced into official receivership.
3. Approximately 42,000 Euro.
4. *Dreamhack* is the world's largest digital festival consisting of a series of events in different countries, while the *Roskilde* music festival is arranged annually in Denmark.
5. Caravan Club of Sweden is an organization for caravanners that run both campsites and activities. In 2016 the club had 30,000 member families all over Sweden.

REFERENCES

Aspers, Patrik, and Asaf Darr. 2011. "Trade Shows and the Creation of Market and Industry." *The Sociological Review* 59(4): 758–778.

Cheng, Yi'en. 2014. "Telling Stories of the City Walking Ethnography, Affective Materialities and Mobile Encounters." *Space and Culture* 17(3): 211–223.

Daniels, Inge. 2009. "Seasonal and Commercial Rhythms of Domestic Consumption. A Japanese Case Study." In *Time, Consumption and Everyday Life. Practice, Materiality and Culture*, eds. Elisabeth Shove, Frank Trentmann, and Richard Wilk. Oxford: Berg.

Elliot, Alice, Roger Norum, and Noel Salazar. 2017. *Methodologies of Mobility: Ethnography and Experiment*. Oxford: Berghahn.

Gudeman, Stephen. 2016. *Anthropology and Economy*. Cambridge: Cambridge University Press.

Hart, Keith. 1973. "Informal Income Opportunities and Urban Employment in Ghana." *The Journal of Modern African Studies* 11(1): 61–89.

Hart, Keith. 2005. *The Hitman's Dilemma: Or Business, Personal and Impersonal*. Chicago: University of Chicago Press for Prickly Paradigm Press.

Hart, Keith. 2006. "Bureaucratic Form and the Informal Economy." In *Linking the Formal and Informal Economy: Concepts and Policies*, eds. B. Guha-Khasnobis, R. Kanbur, and E. Ostrom. Oxford: Oxford University Press.

Ingold, Tim, and Jo Vergunst (eds.). 2008. *Ways of Walking: Ethnography and Practice on Foot*. London: Routledge.

Lampel, Joseph, and Alan D. Meyer. 2008. "Field-Configuring Events as Structuring Mechanisms: How Conferences, Ceremonies, and Trade Shows Constitute New Technologies, Industries, and Markets." *Journal of Management Studies* 45: 1025–1035.

Leivestad, Hege Høyer. 2015. *Lives on Wheels: Caravan Homes in Contemporary Europe*. PhD diss. Department of Social Anthropology. Stockholm: Stockholm University.

Leivestad, Hege Høyer. 2017. "Inventorying Mobility: Methodology on Wheels." In *Methodologies of Mobility: Ethnography and Experiment*, eds. Alice Elliott, Roger Norum, and Noel Salazar. Oxford: Berghahn.

Moeran, Brian, and Jesper Strandgaard Pedersen. 2011. *Negotiating Values in the Creative Industries: Fairs, Festivals and Competetive Events*. Cambridge: Cambridge University Press.

Shove, Elizabeth, Frank Trentman, and Richard Wilk. 2009. "Introduction." In *Time, Consumption and Everyday Life*, eds. Elizabeth Shove, Frank Trentman, and Richard Wilk. Oxford: Berg.

Skov, Lise. 2006. "The Role of Trade Fairs in the Global Fashion Business." *Current Sociology* 54(5): 764–783.

Wilson, Ara. 2004. *The Intimate Economies of Bangkok. Tomboys, Tycoons and Avon Ladies in the Global City*. Oakland: University of California Press.

CHAPTER 8

Traversing Trade Fairs and Fashion Weeks: On Dependence and Disavowal in the Indian Fashion Industry

Tereza Kuldova

The greater the divide between high and low, the greater the need to police the dividing lines

(Layton 2006: 148–149)

INTRODUCTION: THE ILLUSION OF A SPLIT

India is often portrayed as a country split into two – the world of the rich and the world of the poor, the formal economy and the informal economy, materialism and spirituality, modernity/future and tradition/ past, the "new" versus the "real" India (Kuldova 2016e). Both are

The book chapter was written as part of the research project "Enterprise of Culture: International Structures and Connections in the Fashion Industry" financially supported by the HERA Joint Research Program, under grant agreement no 291827.

T. Kuldova (✉)
Department of Archaeology, Conservation and History, University of Oslo, Oslo, Norway

H. Høyer Leivestad, A. Nyqvist (eds.), *Ethnographies of Conferences and Trade Fairs*, DOI 10.1007/978-3-319-53097-0_8

alternatively cast as either good or bad, depending on context and interest. The business elites can be either despised as the greedy rich or become the only thinkable philanthropic saviours of India–the same quality, greed, is transfigured into benevolence and thus legitimate power (Kuldova 2017). The poor can be alternatively perceived as backward masses that drag the country down or as the noble poor, idealized as the spirit of the Indian nation–both precisely because of their poverty. The Indian fashion industry is split along the same lines: the world of the trade fairs and fashion weeks are meant to appear as completely independent and separate. Academic discourse, too, often reproduces this illusion of a split India consisting of two parallel worlds that do not meet. We can read that once we exit Gurgaon's gated world-class amenities where the rich reside, we are "'back in India' as it were" (Kalyan 2011: 39) or that those living in the gated luxury spaces are said to aspire to live "as though one were rich and lived in New York, London, Paris, Frankfurt or Amsterdam" (Mani 2008: 53). This split is constituted along the lines of class and caste, which correlate with the tendency to position the privileged part of the population into the present and future of postmodernity, and the other into the past and unbreakable shackles of tradition–both praised and resented depending on interest.

Mirroring this illusory split of India, the Indian fashion industry is, too, split into two social fields that are constructed as fields onto themselves–as distinct, autonomous, independent, as having nothing whatsoever to do with each other. This illusory split is however not unique to the Indian industry, to the contrary, it dominates the Western fashion industry (Entwistle and Rocamora 2011). It even may be the case that this split in India is precisely an effect of the Indian fashion industry being itself built on imitation of the Western industry. On one hand, the social field centred around the spectacular fashion weeks (e.g. Lakme Fashion Week, Wills Lifestyle Fashion Week, Amazon India Couture Week) with star designers, celebrities and industrialists filling the glossy magazines, a field indulging in "artification" of fashion (i.e. turning non-art into art) (Kuldova 2015b; Shapiro and Heinich 2012), privileging immaterial value, and cultivating brand fetishism as well as designer and celebrity personality cults. On the other hand, the social field centred around the textile, apparel and garment international trade fairs (esp. India International Garment Fair) that barely make it into the news, except for brief notes on their inauguration by the Minister of Textiles. This split was also identified by McRobbie in the case of British fashion industry, who juxtaposed the notions of "fashion as art" and "fashion as rag trade," pointing to the high symbolic capital of art and low symbolic capital of commerce (Mcrobbie 1998). What is significant here is that the former field is symbolically central to the fashion industry at large, while the latter is economically central. What needs to be made clear from the outset is that this split is not in any way natural or obvious, to the contrary, an enormous amount of social labour goes into producing this split. Throughout this text, I will hence try to show how this split is reproduced and reinforced through trade fairs and fashion weeks, and how it legitimizes existing power and class relations.

The former field, marked by visible symbolic capital of its mediatized protagonists overshadows the latter field marked by concentration of economic capital and large-scale exploitation (Hoskins 2014; Ross 2007). Due to its symbolic power, the former field pushes into invisibility the latter field by privileging the culturally, aesthetically and symbolically powerful art, design and immaterial value over material production and business. The former field also has a tendency to appear as if free of any economic need – a cultural and aesthetic economy (Entwistle 2009), or creative capitalism, in which the underlying economy of manufacturing is systematically disavowed. This split is further enhanced by the old/new division which parallels the imaginary tradition/modernity split of India at large. As opposed to the young and heavily mediated high fashion field (Khaire 2011; Kuldova 2016e; Sandhu 2014; Varma 2015) – the Fashion Design Council of India was established first in 1998 and the first fashion week took place in 2000, organized by the same body – the field structured around textile and apparel manufacturing employs millions of artisans and has a long tradition in India (Calico museum 1971; Crill 2006, Crill 2010; Gillow and Barnard 2008; Kumar 2006; Maskiell 1999; Tyabji 2007).

Fashion weeks and garment trade fairs are theorized here along the lines of Bourdieu's field theory in general (Bourdieu 1984, 1985, 1996) and in particular as "field-configuring events" as proposed by Skov and Meier (Skov and Meier 2011: 271). This entails the idea that the respective social fields, with their internal status hierarchies, prestige mechanisms, habitus and related means of acquiring social, symbolic and cultural capital, and organized according to the overall value and composition of capital (Bourdieu 1985), are reinforced and reproduced precisely during such events. However, while there has been research done on the internal workings of social fields of high fashion on one hand–Rocamora and

Entwistle have for instance analyzed well the internal organization of the social field structured around the London Fashion Week (Entwistle and Rocamora 2011)–and of the garment trade shows on the other–the work of Skov is instructive here (Skov 2006)–there has been no discussion of how these social fields relate to each other. Even if both types of events are organized to attract major buyers, it is the publically largely invisible trade shows that result in business deals worth millions–unlike the mediated and heavily sponsored elitist events that remain a niche market. However, the economically marginal (fashion weeks) becomes symbolically central for the industry at large–a general principle often at work in social life (Stallybrass and White 1986).

This illusory split is further discursively reproduced in popular glossy magazines, which feed off and construct the symbolic power of high fashion with the figure of the creative designer at its centre (Kim 1998). Even here the academic discourse is not innocent. Fashion studies have been privileging the top segment of the industry and the star designers (Geczy and Gonzales 2010; Jansen 2015; Karaminas 2012; Kawamura 2005; Müller 2000; Puwar 2002; Sandhu 2014; Troy 2003; Tsui 2010; Wu 2009) over theorizing interdependencies within the industry as a whole. On the opposite end of the academic spectrum we find historicizing texts focusing on diverse textile traditions and traditional crafts, but even here, this research field has shied away from connecting craft to industry, manufacturing and to top designers (Crill 2006, 2010; Gillow and Barnard 2008; Irwin and Hall 1973; Kumar 2006; Tyabji 2007). The same prioritization and thus also reinforcement of the symbolically central over the economically dominant is visible in the rise of fashion exhibitions across prestigious museums around the globe. These curated exhibitions typically focus on selected star designers and their creations, which are then exhibited as art pieces (Kuldova 2014; Melchior and Svensson 2014; Steele 2008) typically robbed of any context of production. Gornostaeva Rieple and Barnes have argued along similar lines when showing that "cultural theorists seem to consider apparel manufacturing to be inferior to, and analyzed separately from, the fashion designing process" (Gornostaeva et al. 2014: 6). Hence, not only glossy magazines, but also academic writing, especially the emerging fashion studies, has been complicit in actively reproducing the split between these social fields by under-theorizing and neglecting the existing interdependencies and economic interests of the industry, that is "under-communicating" the fact that it is primarily business, and "over-communicating" (Goffman 1969) its statistically marginal artistic ambitions, thus further reinforcing them as symbolically central features of the industry as a whole. The hyper-focus on theorizing the work and role of individual fashion designers, of their collections on the ramp, and the very high end of the industry, together with the cultivation of the romantic idea of a fashion designer as an artist and creative genius (Kuldova 2016d) is in practice actively contributing to the production of symbolic dominance of the social field of high fashion and the symbolic power relations, in effect pushing the economic structures underlying the industry into invisibility (Hoskins 2014; Kuldova 2016d) while also authorizing self-interested namings of the top level of the industry. Glossy magazines, as much as the repetitive citationality (Nakassis 2013) of academic discourses about high fashion possess the "capacity to make entities exist in the explicit state, to publish, make public (i.e., render objectified, visible, and even official)," a capacity that "represents a formidable social power, the power to make groups by making the *common sense*, the explicit consensus, of the whole group" (Bourdieu 1985: 729), thus providing, crucially, legitimacy to the split. In my own work, I have attempted to transgress this illusory split by following the commodity, in my case embroidered garments, from production in remote villages to fashion ramps, analyzing the relations of production in the process (Kuldova 2016c, 2016e).

Here, the goal, as mentioned earlier, is to analyze the reproduction and reinforcement of the split itself through the formative events of fashion weeks and trade fairs, and the ways in which the split legitimizes existing relations of power, while being also formative of professional identities. Against the hegemonic cultivation of the split between these social fields, we must insist on the real existence of only one field and only one value chain, within which all actors are inevitably plugged. Within this one field, players are dependent on each other, co-operate against this illusory divide and generate economic, cultural and symbolic capital, but also rob certain players within the industry of the possibility of generating any of the aforementioned capitals. In other words, we must insist that the material boundaries of a field do not necessarily coincide with the imaginary boundaries. This is not to say that the imaginary boundaries do not have profound effects on structuring realities on ground, to the contrary. Hence, taking as the starting point the recognition of the material and economic relations of the Indian fashion industry at large, I will attempt here to break with these established reifying narratives and instead show how the split between the social fields of high fashion and garment manufacturing is constituted and (re)produced in practice. Moreover, I will argue that this split functions as: (a) a legitimization of existing power relations, (b) strategic valorization and devaluation of actors and of their production driven by the economic interest of the dominant players and finally (c) as a means of pushing the economic structures of exploitation into invisibility.

In order to pursue the argument sketched above, I will use the example of the Indian fashion industry, which I have extensively studied ethnographically (Kuldova 2013a, 2013b, 2015a, 2015b, 2016a, 2016c, 2016d, 2016e), as it provides a unique perspective on how elitist fashion circles relate to the realms of manufacturing, something that is more intensely visible precisely because of the aesthetic dependence of Indian fashion designers on hundreds of thousands of creative artisans, weavers and other workforce–the dominant trend of the industry is "royal chic" (Kuldova 2013c), which revels in heritage, craft and opulence. The case of the Indian fashion industry is also particularly interesting because of the youth of the high-end fashion segment and because of India being imagined on the global map as the place of cheap labor, a place of material production rather than a place of artistic and immaterial production. This, together with the aforementioned dependency of the Indian fashion designers on the craftspeople across India, puts the field structured around the fashion weeks into a very specific predicament. Namely, into a state of excessive need to legitimize the artificial boundary between the fields; the need to legitimize the split becomes more pronounced when these fields co-exist so obviously within one country (unlike with the majority of western fashion, in which material production is outsourced abroad to cheaper production locations, wherein the West can be positioned as either the exploiter or the savior of the East).

Fashion weeks and trade fairs are essential to the processes of legitimization as well as being important locations "for intensive boundary work. During social interactions at the show, distinctions were made between those in and outside the markets" (Aspers and Darr 2011: 775). Access to elite events such as fashion weeks is limited only to sponsors, selected buyers, celebrities and elite clients, journalists, bloggers and hired personnel. The prestige and symbolic capital of the most visible players – designers, celebrities, elite clients, and sponsoring brands–is mutually reinforced within the enclosed space of the temporary elitist event. The fashion weeks, as well as trade fairs, can be conceived as "tournament rituals" (Anand and Jones 2008; Anand and Watson 2004) through which fields are configured, as rituals which function as "political symbols that are fabricated and controlled by interested and motivated actors or ritual entrepreneurs whose aim is to influence field configuration" (Moeran and Pedersen 2011: 20). However, "the legitimacy and taken-for-grantedness of ritual is not given, but is an ongoing accomplishment that organizers of the ritual have to constantly strive for" (Anand and Jones 2008: 1057). The illusory split thus has to be repetitively re-enacted, in particular through re-staging of the fashion weeks, which hold a far greater legitimizing and symbolic power. This power imbalance is also mirrored in the funding structure of these two types of field-configuring events are funded from different sources–fashion weeks are sponsored by private international and national players (e.g. Amazon, Maybelline, Nokia, DHL, Reliance etc.), while trade fairs are typically organized by governmental bodies, such as the Ministry of Textiles and Ministry of Commerce in association with diverse export and manufacturing associations, and are designed to attract international economic capital. While this makes the split appear "natural," we have to insist that it has been "naturalized" against better knowledge (a knowledge of interdependence). Hence, what we are dealing here with are rather integrated structures of disavowal, where one field disavows the other, against the reality being well integrated and pursuing the same goals. Positing the interdependence of these fields is not any revelation of well-hidden truth–to the contrary, we all know all too well that fashion is not really high art, but a cut-throat exploitative business (in which, in addition to the modern sweatshop slavery, even the creative professionals are increasingly self-exploiting themselves) and one of leading causes of environmental destruction–still, we prefer to believe the former and enjoy fashion, freed of guilt. The split between the social fields thus helps us cultivate a self-deception in face of accurate perception, a perception of an increasingly traumatic reality of global rise of socio-economic inequality and exploitation inherent to consumer products. Layton argues that this "capacity to hallucinate a way out of painful tension and inevitable environmental disappointments (the breast cannot always be there) can be a source of creativity, to be sure. But when that capacity becomes a regularly practiced disavowal of the truth of dependence, interdependence and vulnerability, we have the makings of a perverse situation" (Layton 2010: 310). However, I would argue that the problem is not as simple as the disavowal of the truth, or the reality, such as the reality of the interdependence, but that instead, we are dealing here with a disavowal of the illusion (not of the reality) of the split– we shall return to this point.

In case of the "western" fashion industry, dislocation of production enables a natural boundary maintenance between the fields centred around fashion weeks and those centred around trade fairs. The symbolic capital follows also this geographic division, and resides primarily with the fashion centres in the West (Milan, Paris, London, New York), a cultural economy of western cities (Scott 2000) that are associated with creative industries, immaterial labour, and design, as well as being the home of the fashion shows, while the East, associated with economic capital, production, manufacture, manual labour and cast as largely unimaginative and imitative (Said 1979), experiences rise in trade fairs (Bathelt 2014; Skov 2006). Even the trade fairs within the West, such as for instance Interstoff in Frankfurt, are increasingly events where the Eastern suppliers come to the West as the numbers of western manufacturers decrease. It is revealing to note that the split of the fields within the fashion industry in the West has gone so far that for instance recent fashion design graduates in London fail to grow, largely because they fail at sourcing and manufacturing. As Gornostaeva Rieple and Barnes note the designers' "participation in manufacturing networks and relationships with manufacturers, whether British or international, lack the necessary levels of trust, reciprocity and knowledge exchange for prototyping and scaling up of production to be achieved effectively" (Gornostaeva et al. 2014: 2), moreover these relations are marked by resentment pertaining largely to the extreme status differences, further leading to unproductive relations.

This makes the Indian case even more interesting, as the fields are co-existing within the same geographical space, which makes it hard for high fashion to claim difference and legitimize its own existence, and thus pushes its discourse of difference to the forefront. The crafts, Indian heritage and the "work" of thousands of indigenous artisans are the staple of Indian couture. Hence, the task of Indian couture is to transform their "work" into an "art of luxury," something that can only occur when the garments are dissociated from the actual origins of their material production, and placed on the ramp, where they are re-cast as luxury artworks and an expression of "artistic nationalism" (Ciotti 2012; Kuldova 2016e) that seeks to turn the "Make in India," also an initiative of the Narendra Modi government to encourage multinational and national companies to manufacture in India, into a synonym with quality and luxury and dissociate it from cheap labour–at the same time as thousands of artisans that work, also, for the high end designers struggle below and little above the poverty line. Speaking about the upcoming

India Couture Week 2016 in New Delhi, Sunil Sethi, the president of the Fashion Design Council of India, remarked:

> We have always offered the best of India through our eponymous events and the ICW is the most coveted extravaganza in the stable as it showcases couture ensembles, which are emblematic of our rich tradition and historical past. As we get set to indulge in this unadulterated visual treat, we hope to recreate splendor through the art of luxury.[1]

The discourse employed here by Sunil Sethi is crucial in boundary maintenance. In this respect, the genre of press releases/reporting in the two fields is also revealing. On one hand we have the fashion week press releases, focusing on creativity and individual designers and on the other the trade fair reports, with detailed statistics and reporting on economic discussions, disavowing creativity altogether. A simple juxtaposition of (1) an excerpt from a press release of the Lakme Fashion Week (LFW) Summer/Resort Season 2014[2] with (2) an excerpt from the 56th India International Garment Fair (January 20–22nd, 2016)[3] reveals the obvious differences between the discourses that pertain to these fields:

> (1) As Lakmé Fashion Week (LFW), India's leading fashion trade event enters in its fifteenth year, it's proud to present yet another exciting Summer/Resort season. LFW today announced a robust line-up of 98 participating designers and 13 sponsors who have come together to celebrate the very best of fashion and creative talent. Over the years, Lakmé Fashion Week has set new trends, promoted young talent and taken the lead on the digital front for the industry to follow. This season too will witness the industry's most established names come together with young talent to set an unparalleled benchmark of diversity, creativity and energy.

> Purnima Lamba – Head of Innovation at Lakmé said: Each season of Lakmé Fashion Week, we collaborate with the finest fashion designers to bring alive the Lakmé beauty statement through an avant-garde presentation. This season we are infusing the magic of color and light into summer with the Lakmé Absolute Color Illusion range that spells mystery with each stroke of cool metallic shades. We look forward to a spellbinding finale with Rajesh Pratap Singh's interpretation of Illusion in his unique textures.

> (2) During the inaugural address by Sh. Santosh Kumar Gangwar, Hon'ble Minister of State for Textiles (IC) highlighted the need to strengthen the Apparel Export Industry. He expressed his confidence that under the

guidance of Hon'ble Prime Minister of India, the garment export industry would be able to achieve a double-digit growth in the exports shortly. The minister also informed that around Rs. 18 000 crores have been allocated under TUFs Scheme and the scheme would be notified within a week. (...) Smt Rashmi Verma, IAS, Secretary, Ministry of Textiles, stated that technology issues and non-existence of FTA with European Union, US and Canada were the challenges in the way of apparel exports. She highlighted the need for bridging the gap in value chain so that Indian exports comprise of apparels rather than cotton and yarns. (...) Shri Ashok G Rajani Chariman, AEPC during the inauguration ceremony stated that the garment export sector is currently worth about 17, 000 million USD, having a world market share of barely 3,5 per cent. (...) Expressing the concern of the garment export industry Sg. Ashok G. Rajani said that "Exporters are concerned with zero duty access in EU market by Vietnam. Vietnam exports are likely to grow faster due to implementation of zero duty from 2017. (India faces import duty of 9, 6 per cent). The Trans Pacific Partnership Agreement allows export opportunities to Vietnam in USA with a benefit of 17–30 per cent export duty relief. India-EU Broad-based Trade and Investment Agreement (BTIA) are yet to be finalized, exporters are expecting faster conclusion of the talk so they can compete with Bangladesh and Vietnam". (...) Stalls of 322 national participants across all over India were spread over in 6 large halls. (...) 749 quality international buyers from 69 countries and 432 buying agents visited during three days of fair. (...) A Fashion Street was made at Hall no. 12A, wherein the collections of the participants were displayed on the mannequins for the benefit of the visiting buyers.

The trade agreements essential to the Indian fashion industry are discussed during the trade fairs. Critical questions to the trade are discussed both in formal and informal meetings; this is the moment when business meets politics, this one of crucial venues where businessmen can put pressure on politicians to do their bidding. Not only do the fashion weeks not have the same capacity to directly engage in policy, but the celebrity hype around these ritualistic and symbolically powerful events also captures all the interest of the media and as such prevents reporting of information about the important meetings that influence the lives of thousands of workers. Fashion becomes only notoriously superficial, celebrity affair, with occasional bursts of pseudo-political activist performance of care for the environment, or gender issues and so on. The illusory quality of the split and the role of the top players across the fields is clearly visible in the persona of the aforementioned

Sunil Sethi, who, before becoming the president of FDCI, set up in 1988 Alliance Merchandizing, a sourcing and buying company, and is today also the vice-president of Li&Fung Group in India (an international sourcing company that operates across 40 countries). Like any other player within the high-end industry, he is a proof of the integrated nature of these fields. Sethi is also a vocal proponent of the "brand India," intent to show the world India's creativity and skill. The building of a strong brand India is the ultimate goal of Narendra Modi's "Make in India" campaign aimed at changing the perception of India globally, and increasing and easing foreign investment.

THE DISAVOWED ILLUSION OF A SPLIT

Now that we have dealt with the illusion of the split and the multiple ways in which it is reproduced, I want us to look closer at the structure of disavowal which it entails. In order to do this, I shall focus on the relationship between two different classes of social actors pertaining to the two fields–(a) high-end *fashion designers* and (b) *manufacturers*, who both individually and through each other hold together vast networks of craftspeople and weavers, a third class of agents, invisible and non-present during trade fairs. By a class of actors, I refer here to the "sets of agents who occupy similar positions and who, being placed in similar conditions and subjected to similar conditionings, have every likelihood of having similar dispositions and interests and therefore of producing similar practices and adopting similar stances" (Bourdieu 1985: 725). This focus on the symbolically and economically crucial actors across the two fields, will also allow us to throw a new light on the *relational* constitution of their professional identities, which pertains here to what Bourdieu called the "work of representation," which has to be constantly performed "in order to impose" one's "view of the world" or of one's view of one's "own position in this world," his or her "social identity" (Bourdieu 1985: 727). In this sense, we shall bracket the obvious elements of the constitution of social identity of the aforementioned actors, such as their individual social background, education, titles, awards, achievements, and so on. We do so, in order to focus solely on the ways in which their identities are shaped by the relationality and by the split between the two fields–thus illuminating a significant part of their identity, one that pertains to relationality, but one that also belongs to the "us versus them" logic. The question pertaining to the professional identities hence is–how does the split between the two fields contribute to forging, shaping, enforcing, and legitimizing the positional value of these identities, as much as the fields themselves?

Even here, at the level of the individual professional self-identifications of the key players, we will be able to observe that the illusion of a split emerges as a "disavowed illusion" (Pfaller 2014). This illusion is predominantly socially reproduced through the work of the field of high fashion and to reiterate, could be put crudely as follows: fashion is art and as such has nothing whatsoever to do with economy. And yet, nobody in the industry, and even possibly outside of it, really believes in it. Nonetheless, this illusion structures the field and (a) enables us to take pleasure in fashion on one hand and (b) reproduces structural violence on the other, the two going uncannily hand in hand. The following excerpts from interviews with (1) a fashion designer or rather a couturier and (2) a manufacturer-cum-merchandizer[4] point to the structure of disavowals crucial to the boundary maintenance between the fields, and read together these excerpts that exemplify the construction of the illusory split, while pointing us to the reality of interdependence of the two fields:

FD: Fashion is art. I will defend this position anytime. I am an artist; I am only interested in making beautiful objects, and nothing else.

TK: Do you not see yourself also as a businessman? Every day you negotiate with clients, buyers, control the production of your designs, control orders to manufacturers and so on?

FD: If you are driven by passion, if you are inspired, if you are always in the creative flow, these things happen on their own, without you even noticing, it just happens. It all expands and grows. It is all part of my creative vision.

TK: But is it not just business? You hire people that source fabrics for you, you hire young designers, accountants, store keepers, buyers, is it not all about money rather than about creativity?

FD: Of course it is business and there is a lot of poverty and exploitation in it too, but fashion is art and for me it is only about creating beauty.[5]

(...)

TK: Do you visit garment trade fairs?

FD: Of course, but for that, I have to dress down, like seriously, so they would not recognize me, though I doubt these people really follow high fashion, at best they only copy pictures from magazines. But it is the same like going to Chandni Chowk or Chor Bazaar, just take some sweatpants and an old t-shirt, you just don't want to look like a top designer. I look what I could buy, some of the manufacturers can do your designs, like very cheaply and in whatever volume you want, some can even export some stuff for you, they have contacts and all, so you can expand to new locations through them, like they offer some services also.[6] So I check them out and make my list, and then I send my person over there. I do not talk to these people myself. I just send someone.... Oh, by the way, have you ever seen the fashion shows they sometimes stage at these fairs? It is an utter disaster, total joke, like some village imitation of a fashion week, total mockery.

TK: So how much of your production is outsourced to such manufacturers?

FD: Percent-wise, I'd say like 80 per cent, maybe even more. All the cheaper stuff we sell, in between 75 – 300USD and of course accessories and all that other stuff.

The manufacturer-cum-merchandizer in the next interview has been attending trade fairs for the last 15 years and his business is 30 years old. If there is anyone that he mistrusts, it is the designers:

M: They send someone, make me invest in sampling and design development, again and again, and then order few pieces while haggling over price. Then they put their brand name on it and charge premium. Ok, everyone does that, I am not selling a brand, but when I sell to Primark or Marks & Spencer, they take more pieces, there is no haggling, they do not put on any premium branded price, it is just clothes, fast fashion as they call it.

TK: Does it bother you that they do not recognize the creativity on your side of the production?

M: Look, for me it is about business, I do not care about creativity, there is more to manufacturing than an idea or a sketch. I am a practical person. But of course it is our designs we sell, we have craftspeople working for us, as well as tailors and so on. You always have to have some new patterns to show, show something different that catches the eye, that is how you get new buyers, you have to have something different, but also, it cannot be too different. Nobody buys crazy. That is the nature of the business, put a new detail here and there, keep the basics the same. It is fashion, there is only so much you can do. But they pay for new detail. They ask for flower patterns, or whatever, we give it to them. All comes from our craftspeople, they do both traditional and modern, like zardozi and we also source some chikankari and we have lot of handwoven fabrics too, but also synthetics, and chiffon is popular. Very few designer houses send us their own patterns, they think we would "steal" them, but they take all patterns from us, but that is not stealing to them, because we are not on that level, but ultimately they pay us for our designs. The problem is often that they accuse us of copying and selling the same thing to others, but it was our design in the first place! They complain we copied it, it was on the street before getting into some magazine, but of course we sell it to others as well. But most of the time, you do not even know who you are working for and where the clothes end up, they are all very secretive about it. With Americans and Europeans, you usually know who you work for, but with Indians, it can be anybody placing orders. But we also had fancy western brands, we did not know we were working for them, then someone saw our clothes in a magazine. But who knows, they put their label on it, and nobody knows who made it. Some put even Made in some European country, on clothes made by us. You know, they stitch couple of extra buttons, or add some design element in a factory in Europe and it counts as made there. Some percentage counts, I do not know, but we have seen that. I cannot worry about that, my business is here, once I sell it, I do not know what happens. . . .

He sells to designers for the same price as to for instance Primark, US$ 2–8 per piece. Throughout the interview he repeats several times that I should understand one thing, namely that it does not matter at all if you buy from a designer or from a fast fashion store, as all the clothes are produced in the end by the same people. In the same factory, he has produced for both Primark and Paul Smith.

    M: The thousands of artisans keep everyone alive, while struggling them-selves. That is the nature of the industry. But the designers think they are better than that, that they are beyond that. But what can I do? They are different kind of people. They have their world and we are not part of it.

   TK: What annoys you most when working with designers?

    M: Arrogance. They pretend like we do not exist, or like we are dirty low people. But it is them nobody really needs, anybody can design clothes. . . . Look, my pieces may be cheap, but that does not make me a cheap person. In fact, I make more money selling to international buyers than most of these designers. Or I don't know how much they earn, but I earn a lot, have several houses, cars, employ more than 2000 people. In the end it is about money, a dirty industry, but at least I am honest about it.

   TK: Do you ever go to fashion weeks?

M: No, everything is online now, whatever designs they make. I am not that class, I can't put up a stand there. I do not talk like them, I am a practical person, business-oriented. What would I do there? In the end they come to me anyway, so why would I go to them?

These excerpts from the conversations with differently positioned players within the fashion industry point us towards the illusionary split, one that here interestingly takes the form of "us versus them" logic (Eriksen 1993). The disavowed illusion here becomes central to the players' professional identity that is to a large degree dependent on belonging to the respective social field.

First, we have encountered the designer, who, like the majority of well-known designers, clearly conceives of his work as art and denies that it has anything to do with business. As Tang notes, following Bourdieu, a "fine work of art must initiate itself as anti- economic for it to be valued as a unique, auratic object or gesture, apparently divorced from crude forces of instrumentalization" (Tang 2011: 75). Even in India the "design-speak" (Kuldova 2016e) of the high-end industry considers, much like in the West, manufacturing "to be responsible for just 'a simple input' into the symbolic fashion product. What is emblematic is that almost no industry commentators from within the fashion field include manufacturers in their descriptions of the fashion industry. However, without this input (...) this product cannot be made, legitimized and reproduced" (Gornostaeva et al. 2014: 12). This is an even more paradoxical move considering that he is a successful businessman and that being a successful businessman (Varma 2015) is highly valorized *inside* the field centered around fashion weeks; in particular, in front of the business elite clients and (inter)national buyers it becomes an additional means of acquiring respect within the field. Towards the outside, however, it seems imperative to insist on strict dissociation from business, something we can observe also very clearly in the Western fashion industry (Entwistle and Rocamora 2011). His self-identified professional identity is constructed solely around the ramp lime-light covered by the media, where fashion is displayed as art for the consumption of the super-rich, staged in a theatrical and ritualistic environment.

Since the field structured around the fashion weeks is, as we have established, symbolically dominant, it is important to understand the structure of disavowal that occurs here, which reflects the relations of power in the industry. At first, the couturier denies the reality of fashion being a business and with it also the whole field structured around trade fairs; trade fairs are considered as pure business venues, where international buyers look for economically viable and trustworthy suppliers, venues that have little to do with creativity. But already here we can observe the ambiguity of this relation as he confesses to visit trade fairs undercover in search of manufacturers and suppliers from around India. And he is not alone, the practice of top-down "espionage" appears to be widespread, as several designers told me – it is a bit like appropriating street fashion of the poor in India, only getting it manufactured and sometimes even exported at the same time. Dressing down in order to visit trade fairs also suggests that he considers them lowly, by definition not for people like him. The fashion shows presented at the trade fairs are a clear mockery to him, even though it is clear that the intention of the organizers of the trade fairs is to include series of more prestigious events into the trade fair program, precisely by capitalizing on the symbolic power of couture.

Following his own self-definition, the fashion designer clearly first positions business as something irrelevant, and secondly as something low, or rather as something below him. At first, he even denies the reality of fashion being a business. However, immediately after that, we see that he acknowledges that fashion is indeed, often even a dirty, business—"everyone knows that!." It is thus not that he does not know that fashion is business, or that he does not know that he himself is primarily a capitalist, employing more than hundred people directly and possibly several thousand indirectly each month, while capitalizing on his image as a creative genius, being at the same time himself a commodity to be consumed. As he himself said: "Of course it is business and there is a lot of poverty and exploitation in it too, but fashion is art and for me it is only about creating beauty." This suggests the aforementioned structure of disavowal, where it is not primarily the reality that is disavowed, but instead the illusion – in our case the illusion of the split itself. The structure of disavowal in respect to illusions, has been brilliantly analyzed by Robert Pfaller, who has labelled them as "illusions without owners" (Pfaller 2014) and recognized such illusions as sources of cultural pleasure. Even in this case, the illusion of the split of the industry, a split between the creative and seductive field of fashion as art, and the exploitative business on the other hand, functions as a source of cultural pleasure, both for the practitioners and consumers—be it of the clothes themselves or of their mediated images. The illusion itself can also stimulate creativity across the industry at large. But it is also a source of pleasure, I would argue, in that it relieves us from thinking about the conditions of production of fashion at large, precisely by maintaining the illusory boundary between the two social fields–in which nobody believes, and yet we collectively act as if the boundary was real.

On the other side of the illusory split, the manufacturer-cum-merchandizer's self-definition emerges in opposition to the designer's, as he fully and explicitly embraces his identity as a businessman–a result of the antagonistic relations between the fields. And yet, the question of creativity remains ambiguous for him. It is clear that the creativity of the people employed by him, and even his own, is totally denied precisely by relegating the whole field into a matter of dirty and utilitarian business. This, I believe, is also partially an effect of neoliberal restructuring of the industry that, in this case, merges with pre-existing class and caste structures. As Layton has remarked, in an "increasingly individualist meritocracy, a few people are recognized as truly talented, and the rest are relegated to the non-special status of a disposable mass" (Layton 2010: 310). But the merchandiser also touched upon a central point, and possibly also a traumatic point, especially from the viewpoint of the designer and of the symbolically central field of high fashion, namely dependency. As he said: "But the rest is produced by people like me, we keep the designers alive. The thousands of artisans keep everyone alive, while struggling themselves." It is precisely this dependency that needs to be denied, the dependency of the actors on each other, the dependency of one field on the other, and thus their inability to be operate on their own. As Layton (2010: 305) remarked:

> The first occurrence of disavowal in our lives, according to Freud (1900), appears as a resistance to acknowledging the reality of dependence on others. The hungry baby, who has no control over the appearance or disappearance of the mother, hallucinates the breast, thus finding an omnipotent solution to a painful reality: I don't need you; I'm self-sufficient.

It is not a coincidence that narratives of individualism, creative genius and personality cults dominate the self-presentations of leading fashion designers. After all, contemporary business too is dominated by narratives of "self-made" billionaires. The denial of dependency and interdependency is also a denial of complicity (but also of vulnerability), which results in a social perversion particular to the neoliberal era (Layton 2010).

Disavowed Illusion as Source of Cultural Pleasure and Structural Violence

This brief exposition was motivated by the pressing need to reconnect, in theory, the in practice interdependent fields of the fashion industry, fields that remain too often theoretically, as well as popularly, kept separate. As such, the first step towards an integrated theory of the fashion industry is, according to me, understanding the way in which the split between the fields has been constituted. The split of the industry, which is at large shaped by the field-configuring events of fashion weeks and trade fairs, is, as I have tried to show, not automatic, obvious, or natural. Instead, this split is naturalized and demands re-productive labour on the part of the respective players within the industry in order to be sustained–a re-productive labour in which, as we have seen, academic discourse becomes also unintentionally complicit. The ritualistic, temporary and spatially bounded events, the fashion weeks and trade fairs, are essential to the work of naturalization and justification of social stratification, and of structural violence inherent to the industry–a violence without which the industry, at present stage, cannot be thought. Even the businessmen, who exhibit at the trade fairs and who are befriended with the Minister of Textiles, and thus even against their valuable political connections, assume a submissive position in respect to the field of high fashion. These rituals exert control through mystification and force ideological conformity (Roth 1995), not only on the participants, but also on actors within the industry who do not belong to the exclusive gated circles, and on the worldwide consumers of the images of these events.

The disavowed illusion of the split, which has been identified here, the illusion that nobody seems to believe in (Pfaller 2014), yet one that structures the real relations on the ground, serves two main functions–in addition to providing different actors within the industry with hierarchical status position and self-definitions. Namely, it is, as any "illusion without owners," a source of cultural pleasure, in this case even of creativity, possibly even of sublimation. As such, this illusion can not only stimulate creativity on part of the privileged creatives, but also relieve them, as much the consumers, of thinking about the conditions of production. The illusion enables the designers as much as real and virtual consumers of fashion to take pleasure in fashion, to consider it aesthetically, to consider it elevating. This is certainly a cultural achievement that has to be celebrated, an achievement of culture that needs to be sustained–its ability to sublimate painful reality into a work of art. However, we must also insist that this disavowed illusion is not only a source of pleasure, of creativity, of culture, but that it is also instrumental in the reproduction of structural violence on the ground. Here we could argue that the fact that the illusion of the split is a public secret, something everyone knows but few systematically articulate in public debate, paradoxically intensifies the mystification or obfuscation. Precisely because we know better we fall for the trap even harder, against our cynical distance (Kuldova 2016b). With Žižek we could even consider this disavowed illusion as fetish, as an "embodiment of the lies that enables us to sustain the unbearable truth" (Žižek 2007: 251). The disavowed illusion thus also reproduces the existing structural violence along with the relations of exploitation, making them at the same time more bearable. If nothing else, this is the perverse beauty of the fashion weeks.

Notes

1. http://mediaindia.eu/art-culture/india-couture-week-2016-begins-on-july-20-in-new-delhi/ (accessed July 8, 2016).
2. The full press release can be accessed here: http://pressreleasewatch.blog spot.co.at/2014/03/lakme-fashion-week-lfw-summerresort.html (accessed May 10, 2016).
3. The full report can be accessed here: http://indiaapparelfair.com/pdf/ 56th-IIGF-Report-2016-January.pdf (accessed June 20, 2016).
4. The informal interviews were conducted in 2011 in New Delhi and reconstructed based on field notes, as well as edited for flow, while keeping the original meaning. The second interview was conducted during the 47th India International Garment Fair, July 12–14, 2011.
5. Excerpt from an interview with an Indian fashion designer, November 2011.
6. Businesses such as for instance the Delhi-based Amattra Exports offer services to designer labels that range from manufacturing (pattern making, digitizing, grading, sample machining, fabric advice, production to export). The increasing emergence of such firms further suggests the taking hold of the split in the industry, where the designers are increasingly unskilled in terms of organizing their label and business.

References

Anand, Narasimhan, and Brittany C. Jones. 2008. "Tournament Rituals, Category Dynamics, and Field Configuration: The Case of the Booker Prize." *Journal of Management Studies* 45(6): 1036–1060.

Anand, Narasimhan, and Mary R. Watson. 2004. "Tournament Rituals in the Evolution of Fields: The Case of the Grammy Awards." *The Academy of Management Journal* 47(1): 59–80.

Aspers, Patrik, and Asaf Darr. 2011. "Trade Shows and the Creation of Market and Industry." *Sociological Review* 59(4): 758–778.

Bathelt, Harald. 2014. "The Development of Trade Fair Ecologies in China: Case Studies from Chengdu and Shanghai." *Environment and Planning A*: 46511–46530.

Bourdieu, Pierre. 1984. *Distinction: A Social Critique of the Judgement of Taste.* London: Routledge & Kegan Paul.

Bourdieu, Pierre. 1985. "The Social Space and the Genesis of Groups." *Theory and Society* 14(6): 732–744.

Bourdieu, Pierre. 1996. *The Rules of Art: Genesis and Structure of the Literary Field.* Stanford, CA: Stanford University Press.

Calico Museum Of Textiles 1971. *Historic Textiles of India at the Calico Museum.* Ahmedabad: Calico Museum.

Ciotti, Manuela. 2012. "Post-colonial Renaissance: 'Indianness', Contemporary Art and the Market in the Age of Neoliberal Capital." *Third World Quarterly* 33(4): 637–655.

Crill, Rosemary (ed.). 2006. *Textiles From India: The Global Trade.* Calcutta: Seagull Books.

Crill, Rosemary. 2010. "The Golden Age of Indian Textile Trade." In *Asian Style: Indian Textiles and Fashion in Britain*, eds. C. Breward, P. Crang, and R. Crill. New Delhi: Bookwise (India) Pvt. Ltd. in association with V&A Publishing.

Entwistle, Joanne. 2009. *The Aesthetic Economy of Fashion: Markets and Values in Clothing and Modelling.* Oxford: Berg.

Entwistle, Joanne, and Agnes Rocamora. 2011. "Between Art and Commerce: London Fashion Week as Trade Fair and Fashion Spectacle." In *Negotiating Values in the Creative Industries: Fairs, Festivals and Competitive Events*, eds. B. Moeran and J. Strandgaard Pedersen. New York/Cambridge: Cambridge University Press.

Eriksen, Thomas Hylland. 1993. *Us and Them in Modern Societies: Ethnicity and Nationalism in Mauritius, Trinidad and Beyond.* Oxford: Oxford University Press.

Geczy, Adam, and Vicky Karaminas. 2012. *Fashion and Art.* London: Bloomsbury Academic.

Gillow, John, and Nicholas Barnard. 2008. *Indian Textiles.* London: Thames & Hudson.

Goffman, Erving. 1969. *The Presentation of Self in Everyday Life.* New York: Doubleday.

Gonzales, Ana Marta. 2010. "On Fashion and Fashion Discourses." *Critical Studies in Fashion and Beauty* 1(1): 65–85.

Gornostaeva, Galina, Aison Rieple, and David Barnes. 2014. "The Role of Networks in Fashion Designing: Disconnect Between Designers and Manufacturers in London." *19th DMI: Academic Design Management Conference, London.* 1–25.

Hoskins, Tansy E. 2014. *Stitched Up: The Anti-Capitalist Book of Fashion.* London: Pluto Press.

Irwin, John, and Margaret Hall. 1973. "Indian Embroideries." In *Historic Textiles of India at the Calico Museum, II.* Ahmedabad: Calico Museum.

Jansen, Angela M. 2015. *Moroccan Fashion: Design, Culture and Tradition.* London: Bloomsbury.

Kalyan, Rohan. 2011. "Fragmentation by Design: Architecture, Finance and Identity." *Grey Room*: 4426–4453.

Kawamura, Yuniya. 2005. *Fashion-ology: An Introduction to Fashion Studies.* Oxford: Berg.

Khaire, Mukhti. 2011. "The Indian Fashion Industry and Traditional Indian Crafts." *Business History Review* 85(2): 345–366.

Kim, Sung Bok. 1998. "Is Fashion Art?." *Fashion Theory: The Journal of Dress, Body and Culture* 2(1): 51–71.

Kuldova, Tereza (ed.). 2013a. *Fashion India: Spectacular Capitalism.* Oslo: Akademika Publishing.

Kuldova, Tereza. 2013b. "Laughing at Luxury: Mocking Fashion Designers." In *Fashion India: Spectacular Capitalism*, ed. T. Kuldova. Oslo: Akademika Publishing.

Kuldova, Tereza. 2013c. "'The Maharaja Style': Royal Chic, Heritage Luxury and the Nomadic Elites." *Fashion India: Spectacular Capitalism*, ed. T. Kuldova. Oslo: Akademika Publishing.

Kuldova, Tereza. 2014. "Fashion Exhibition as a Critique of Museum Fashion Exhibitions: The Case of 'Fashion India: Spectacular Capitalism.'" *Critical Studies in Fashion and Beauty* 5(2): 313–336.

Kuldova, Tereza. 2015a. "Designing Hypermuscular Neoaristocracy: Of Kings, Gangsters and Muscles in Indian Cinema, Fashion and Politics." *Film, Fashion and Consumption* 3(2): 149–156.

Kuldova, Tereza. 2015b. "The Indian Cocktail of Value/s and Desire: On Artification of Whisky and Fashion." In *Objects and Imagination*, eds Ø. Fuglerud and L. Wainwright. Oxford: Berghahn Books.

Kuldova, Tereza. 2016a. "Designing for Zippies: On Commercially Inflected Nationalism and Branded 'Subcultures'." In *Styling South Asian Youth Cultures: Fashion, Media and Society*, eds. R. Dasgupta, L. Begum, and R. Lewis. London: I.B. Tauris Publishing.

Kuldova, Tereza. 2016b. "Directing passions in New Delhi's world of fashion: On the power of ritual and 'illusions without owners'." *Thesis Eleven*. Online First (DOI: 10.1177/0725513616663250): 1–18.

Kuldova, Tereza. 2016c. "Fatalist Luxuries: Of Inequality, Wasting and Anti-Work Ethic in India." *Cultural Politics* 12(1): 110–129.

Kuldova, Tereza. 2016d. "Heads Against Hands and Hierarchies of Creativity: Indian Luxury Embroidery between Craft, Fashion Design and Art." In *Creativity in Transition: Politics and Aesthetics of Circulating Images*, eds. M. Svašek and B. Meyer. Berghahn Books.

Kuldova, Tereza. 2016e. *Luxury Indian Fashion: A Social Critique*. London: Bloomsbury.

Kuldova, Tereza. 2017. "Forcing 'Good' and the Legitimization of Informal Power: Philanthrocapitlism and Artistic Nationalism among the Indian Business Elite." *Asienforum: International Quarterly for Asian Studies* 1–12.

Kumar, Ritu. 2006. *Costumes and Textiles of Royal India*. New Delhi: Antique Collectors' Club.

Layton, Lynne. 2006. "Retaliatory Discourse: The Politics of Attack and Withdrawal." *International Journal of Applied Psychoanalytic Studies* 3(2): 143–155.

Layton, Lynne. 2010. "Irrational Exuberance: Neoliberal Subjectivity and the Perversion of Truth." *Subjectivity*: 3303–3322.

Mani, Lata. 2008. "The Phantom of Globality and the Delirium of Excess." *Economic and Political Weekly* 43(39): 41–47.

Maskiell, Michelle. 1999. "Embroidering the Past: Phulkari Textiles and Gendered Work as 'Tradition' and 'Heritage' in Colonial and Contemporary Punjab." *The Journal of Asian Studies* 58(2): 361–388.

Mcrobbie, Angela. 1998. *British Fashion Design*. London: Routledge.

Melchior, Marie Riegels, and Birgitta Svensson (eds.). 2014. *Fashion and Museums: Theory and Practice*. New York: Bloomsbury.

Moeran, Brian, and Jesper Strandgaard Pedersen. 2011. "Introduction." In *Negotiating Values in the Creative Industries: Fairs, Festivals and Competitive Events*, eds. B. Moeran and J. Strandgaard Pedersen. New York/Cambridge: Cambridge University Press.

Müller, Florence. 2000. *Art and Fashion*. London: Thames & Hudson.

Nakassis, Constantine. 2013. "The Quality of a Copy." In *Fashion India: Spectacular Capitalism*, ed. T. Kuldova. Oslo: Akademika Publishing.

Pfaller, Robert. 2014. *On the Pleasure Principle in Culture: Illusions without Owners*. London: Verso.

Puwar, Nirmal. 2002. "Multicultural Fashion...Stirring of Another Sense of Aesthetics and Memory." *Feminist Review*: 7163–7187.

Ross, Robert J. S. 2007. *Slaves to Fashion: Poverty and Abuse in the New Sweatshops*. Ann Arbor: The University of Michigan Press.

Roth, Andrew L. 1995. "'Men Wearing Masks': Issues of the Description in Analysis of Ritual." *Sociological Theory* 13(3): 13201–13227.

Said, Edward W. 1979. *Orientalism*. New York: Vintage Books.

Sandhu, Arthi. 2014. *Indian Fashion: Tradition, Innovation, Style.* London: Bloomsbury.

Scott, Allen J. 2000. *The Cultural Economy of Cities: Essays on the Geography of Image-Producing Industries.* London: Sage.

Shapiro, Roberta, and Heinich. Nathalie. 2012. "When is Artification?" *Contemporary Aesthetics* 4: 101–120. http://www.contempaesthetics.org/newvolume/pages/article.php?articleID=639

Skov, Lise. 2006. "The Role of Trade Fairs in the Global Fashion Business." *Current Sociology* 54(5): 764–783.

Skov, Lise, and Janne Meier. 2011. "Configuring Sustainability at Fashion Week." In *Negotiating Values in the Creative Industries: Fairs, Festivals and Competitive Events*, eds. B. Moeran and J. Strandgaard Pedersen. Cambridge: Cambridge University Press.

Stallybrass, Paul, and Allon. White. 1986. *The Politics and Poetics of Transgression.* London: Methuen.

Steele, Valerie. 2008. "Museum Quality: The Rise of the Fashion Exhibition." *Fashion Theory* 12(1): 7–30.

Tang, Jeannine. 2011. "Biennalization and Its Discontents." In *Negotiating Values in the Creative Industries: Fairs, Festivals and Competitive Events*, eds. B. Moeran and J. Strandgaard Pedersen. Cambridge: Cambridge University Press.

Troy, Nancy J. 2003. *Couture Culture: A Study in Modern Art and Fashion.* Cambridge: MIT Press.

Tsui, Christine. 2010. *China Fashion: Conversations with Designers.* Oxford: Berg.

Tyabji, Laila. 2007. *Threads & Voices: Behind the Indian Textile Tradition.* Published for Marg Publications on behalf of the National Centre for the Performing Arts.

Varma, Meher. 2015. *Making Designs on Fashion: Producing Contemporary Indian Aesthetics.* PhD, University of California, Los Angeles.

Wu, Juanjuan. 2009. *Chinese Fashion: From Mao to Now.* Oxford: Berg Publishers.

Žižek, Slavoj. 2007. "Afterword: With Defenders Like These, Who Needs Attackers?" *The Truth of Žižek*, eds. P. Bowman and R. Stamp. London: Continuum.

INDEX

© The Author(s) 2017
H. Høyer Leivestad, A. Nyqvist (eds.), *Ethnographies of Conferences and Trade Fairs*, DOI 10.1007/978-3-319-53097-0